Between the Mountains
and the Gantries

Published in 2006 by
Appletree Press Ltd
The Old Potato Station
14 Howard Street South
Belfast
BT7 1AP

Tel: +44 (0) 28 90 24 30 74
Fax: + 44 (0) 28 90 24 67 56
Email: reception@appletree.ie
Web: www.appletree.ie

Desk Editor: Jean Brown
Editorial work: Jim Black
Designer: Stuart Wilkinson
Production Manager: Paul McAvoy

Printed and bound in Italy by Grafica Veneta S.p.A.

Between the Mountains and the Gantries

ISBN-10: 0 86281 851 6
ISBN-13: 978 0 86281 851 7

9 8 7 6 5 4 3 2 1

AP3372

Between the Mountains
and the Gantries

Will Morrison

Appletree Press

To my daughters:
Grace, Clare and Sarah
and their children

CONTENTS

Life is lived forwards and understood backwards.

— Soren Kierkegaard

PREFACE

These stories began with an impulse, or you might say, a push. Friends and colleagues had organised a retirement party in my honour, and knowing that I would be expected to give a speech, I was in a quandary as to what I should speak about. At an informal gathering on my last day at the college where I had taught for twenty-two years, I had made a speech in which I had said the appreciative things one says on such an occasion about teaching and students, college and colleagues, with an anecdote here and there to flavour the stew.

It had occurred to me during the closing days of my working life, that my retirement would take effect on a day almost fifty years since the day, as a boy of fourteen years, I began my working life. So, why not tell a story about that year, I said to myself, which in more ways than one, was eventful for me. That story became, with a bit of revising and polishing in the weeks after the party, 'The Launch', and in effect, launched the others that followed. Originally, the stories were for my family circle of children, grandchildren, siblings and their children. But the circle widened to include friends who read them from time to time in typescript as I finished them and enjoyed them.

The stories are a memoir of childhood, in a voice that shifts between the adult and the boy, and in one case, 'Beyond the Beyond' entirely in a young boy's voice. For some of them, I have wrought a single narrative, for others I have adopted the style of the personal essay. Because memoirs are also social documents, I have built into each story, as accurately as I can, descriptions of places and customs, idioms of speech, and dialect. Since memory is tricky, elusive, even illusory, I make no pretence to total recall nor infallible accuracy. Where I may get a detail or fact wrong or partly wrong, I stand to be corrected, as literally I used to be, standing beside my desk in elementary school.

In so far as memoir is a record of the self at certain stages in its growth, it is like an old fading snapshot; certain forms remain distinct but one's features have begun to blur. Psychologists tell us that it is impossible to be absolutely truthful about one's past experience; the censor within, for reasons hidden deep in one's psyche, will block memory from revealing the whole truth. But then, the whole truth is an ambitious aim, and in this memoir I settle for glimpses of truth, and claim no more than that.

The events recorded did happen, but occasionally I have added material, such as sensory impressions, remembered feelings, and minor events which come from other times and places, into a single narrative to enrich the story's texture, as occurs in fiction. Saint Augustine wrote somewhere, 'Everything that is made up is not a lie.' And he should know, having written *Confessions,* the first notable work of autobiography in our western literary tradition.

Of course, from those years I cannot recall verbatim conversations I heard or took part in. So, where I use dialogue, I am inventing as one does in fiction, but the invention consists of words and phrases which I remember would have been used in the circumstances narrated in the stories.

L.P. Hartley noted in his novel, *The Go-Between* 'The past is a foreign country; they do things differently there.' That's especially true when one has spent more than half of one's life in a country quite different from the place of one's childhood. My childhood was another world, not only quite different in landscape and culture from the one I now inhabit but also from the one in which my own children grew up. The more I remember of my childhood, the more its "foreignness" – the incidents, the events, the customs, and even the physical setting and speech of the inhabitants – seems worth preserving in words.

In returning to that past, which is my beginning, I am returning to the world out of which I have invented myself. But the impulse to continue writing stories after 'The Launch' has not been solely in pursuit of self-knowledge. That sort of thing can get out of hand, and to tell you the truth, I have just wanted to tell a good story.

Will Morrison
Burnaby, British Columbia

LOCAL TERMS

borstal boys	boys sent to reform school for committing petty crimes
clabber	mud; sometimes a mix of mud and manure
clarty	dirty or matted with dirt
clutey	left-handed
duncher	a soft cap, characteristic head wear of working men
dunt	a sharp, sudden shove or knock
feg	cigarette
girn	complain
gulder	an exceedingly loud shout
jawbox	a scullery sink
mitching	playing truant
peevers	small heavy square stones once used to pave roads
trammy peevers	peevers laid between tram lines
sheugh	drainage ditch
shillcorn	a festering pimple

Chapter 1

PLUNDERING

FEW PLEASURES on a wet day could match 'plundering'. It required only a pound of curiosity and an ounce of willfulness, and a chest of drawers, wardrobe, and a mysterious travelling trunk.

Our mother assembles her four children in the kitchen:

'I'm goin' out for a wee message, so you mind them childer, Will,' she says to me, and adds a warning, 'An' no plundering.'

Of course, she isn't fifty yards down the street before we are upstairs plundering the two bedrooms – the only two in the house, and the bathroom.

We begin with the dressing table in our parents' bedroom, work through the drawers with the practiced skill of Fagin's apprentices, finger our way through important looking papers. You never know what you might learn about yourself among these papers, I tell myself. Charlie, one of my mates who lived across the street, discovered when plundering, that he was adopted and raced out into the street shouting the good news to anybody who would listen.

But I learn nothing, except when and where I was born, which I knew already, and that my parents, Mabel and William Porter Morrison, are indeed my mother and father, which I never doubted, and that the birth certificate is a "CERTIFIED COPY OF ENTRY OF BIRTH issued for purposes of 'Elementary Education', AND NOT TO BE USED FOR ANY OTHER PURPOSE," signed W.J. Kelly, Asst. Registrar, Twelfth of June, 1933, seventeen days after I make my entry into the world in the upstairs bedroom of number 10 Ballymena Street, Belfast.

You are no sooner born, it seems to me, than you are expected to go to school some day, and if you don't you will have no proof that you were ever born. I check the rent and insurance books to see if there is any change to the rent Mammy pays to the Social Council for our house and how much she has paid to the Prudential Insurance Company in case somebody dies. Penny insurance, she calls it, for funerals. The figures are neat, and I notice that there are no gaps in the columns.

In the bathroom we poke among the towels and linens in the hot press, again find nothing but a little rubber cap and funny looking short rod we can't identify, and then move into our own bedroom to root around the bottom of a huge wardrobe, where Daddy keeps his St John Ambulance First-Aid bag. It holds all sorts and sizes of bandages, rolls of sticking plaster, a bottle of iodine which smells like dulse. For a while we pretend we have broken arms and make slings with square white cloths, then put them back in the bag, folded, but not as neatly as we found them.

We leave the large travelling trunk behind the wardrobe to the last. We have to pull the wardrobe out to be able to open the trunk. On top of the contents lie a few old photographs: Mammy and Daddy on their wedding day, and of Mammy in her Girl Guide uniform. There is a snapshot of Granny Porter which I study intently, trying to fix a picture of her in my mind. I know little about her, because she died when I was four years old. The snapshot shows her with her three grandchildren – my youngest sister, Elsie, is not in it, not yet being born – at the foot of the seawall at Bangor. Norman and Mavis are on her lap, I'm standing, being the tallest and the oldest. Norman and I have buckets and spades. The year is written in the back, 1937, the year before Granny died of throat cancer. There is another photograph, taken in 1939 in Carnmoney Cemetery, of Daddy in his bowler hat, with three of us. Mavis looks shy, Norman looks quizzically at the camera, hands in his tiny overcoat pockets. I am smiling at something happening elsewhere, my hands behind my back like a little man.

We take out of the trunk a long tress of plaited auburn hair that rests between sheets of tissue paper and pass it around, each of us admiring it for its softness and auburn hue. Mammy had long auburn hair before she married. A few old song books and hymn books in tonic solfa lie in a neat pile. There are no names on them. I wonder aloud who once sang the songs and hymns. We riffle through them. I sing some of the tunes, and my brother and sisters giggle. My favourite is 'Poor Black Joe'. I sing all the verses.

Uncle Willie's boxing trunks are neatly folded. He is one of Mammy's two brothers, and is in the Royal Air Force. He joined up when he was seventeen. He is also a boxer. There are two photographs of him. In one he is wearing his uniform, and smiling, in the other he is in his boxing trunks, with his fists up. I pick up the trunks. They have a lovely feel to them, being silk. It will be a few years before they fit me, but even so, I try them on over my trousers, take up a boxer's stance in front of the wardrobe mirror, my fists up, like my Uncle Willie in his photograph. My brother and sisters laugh.

We wonder aloud who wore the Great War regimental cap and belt, puttees, badges, buttons and shoulder insignia, the steel helmet and khaki shorts. Was it Uncle Joe Doyle, Mammy's cousin? Or someone we have never heard of? We agree on Uncle Joe. He is still in the army, in the Royal Ulster Rifles, whose initials are on the insignia. The name, Doyle, is on the trunk. There is a steel helmet in the trunk, but it has no name on it. Doyle is also my dead grandmother's maiden name. There is a book with a lot of names in it, but I recognize only a few of them. Beneath all this stuff lie linens, table cloths, napkins, but we have no interest in them.

Mammy comes home with her messages in her basket.

'Were youse plunderin'agane?' she says after a while.

'Na' we reply in unison.

'I know ye were. What were ye lookin'for?'

'Nathin, Mammy. We weren't lookin'for nothing.'

I wonder how she knows. Or maybe, I think, she is just guessing, since we plunder often.

What were we looking for? Again and again, over the years of our childhood we returned to the trunk behind the wardrobe, knowing in advance what lay there. What did we expect to find each time we raised the heavy lid? Something magical, like the magic in the boxes we read about in fairy tales?

But nothing magical ever happened, and nothing changed, except one day the soldier's cap and badges were no longer there because I had talked Mammy into letting me have them for my war games, and some years later into having the boxing trunks, which Uncle Willie never reclaimed, for I had a fleeting ambition to be a boxer.

Perhaps we just wanted to touch again and again the things that whispered stories; of the long plaited tress, the fading photograph taken in Bangor, of the soldier and the boxer, of the book of names and the singers of the songs, even of the great trunk itself, of the seas and foreign lands it may have crossed; altogether, stories of a mysterious past, but one to which we were connected. Whispers of stories, that's all.

Epilogue

It is a few days after Easter, 1976. My brother and I are in the house on Alliance Road, going through our parents' personal effects, papers, old photographs, mementos stored in the drawers of the dressing table. On Good Friday, we had buried our father, and our mother, unable to take care of herself, will be going to live with my sister. 'Plunderin'agane,' I can hear her saying. This time, though, this last time, we have her permission.

The house is as quiet as the grave.

We don't disturb the trunk behind the wardrobe. It is time to tell our own stories.

Chapter 2

A BURGUNDY LEATHER SCHOOLBAG

IN LATE August of 1939, as Europe lurched toward war, I stepped out as manfully as my short legs could manage for my first day in Senior Infants at Everton Public Elementary School, which was situated where the Crumlin and Ardoyne Roads in North-West Belfast met like a pencil point on the lower slopes of Divis Mountain. I was six years old and allowed, on account of my advanced age, to skip Junior Infants. All I needed to launch my career – a grey slate with faint pale blue lines, on which I would learn to write properly with my graphite stylo, and a yellow twelve-inch ruler with the quarter inches clearly marked – rattled in an old leather schoolbag which hung lopsided from my shoulders.

The schoolbag was a gift to me from one of Mammy's friends whose son had outgrown it. A few scratches criss-crossed its dark burgundy surface, and splotches of ink had stained its stiff leather flap. The right shoulder strap had a tendency to slip as I walked. If I broke into a trot, it would give way entirely, and the bag would twist off my back and swing from the crook of my left arm. But the twin buckles that closed the flap were intact and strong. I had no fear that the bag's contents would spill and scatter across the wet footpath.

A late summer shower had drenched the street, but sunshine was breaking through the thinning membrane of cloud. The privet hedgerows of the little gardens lining the pavement glistened and dripped miniature jewels. Wisps of steam rose from the brown brick faces of rain-washed houses, and curled over wet slate roofs which shone as if they had been polished with floor wax.

I walked to school with Sandy. He was the only child of the Ruddocks,

15

who lived two doors down the street from our house, and like me was starting Senior Infants. His schoolbag, of new bright brown soft leather with shining buckles, hung neatly from his shoulders. I had wanted a new one, too, and had whinged at the prospect of having to carry an old beat-up bag, but Mammy insisted, saying that it would do me until I was in Standard I, at which time she would be able to afford me a new one. On that promise I yielded, but in fact, I had no choice. I didn't know that her frugality arose from necessity. Nor did I know, as I heaved the bag for the umpteenth time into a more comfortable position across my narrow shoulders, that this frugality would govern my needs and wants throughout my boyhood, and enter into the grain of my character.

Sandy's face had such a high colour that I would think that he had been sitting too close to the kitchen fire before he left his house. He had a smile that stretched from ear to ear, but which seemed to make his cheeks look raw, even on that warm August morning, as if they needed a rub of the ointment Mammy smeared around my nostrils when a head cold turned on a tap inside my nose. On the way to school he showed me a trick he could do with his tongue. He curled it upwards until its tip touched his nose. I tried to do it, but failed. I concluded that either my tongue was too short or my nose wasn't low enough down my face. He did his trick for the other pupils in our class, much to their delight, but when his nose ran from a head cold, as it often did, they would grimace, turn away from him, and pretend to vomit. The older boys would only coax him to do his trick when his nose ran, and they would turn to each other and laugh. I knew that they were making fun of him, but I didn't interfere.

None of my classmates coaxed me to show off *my* amazing ability to write with my left hand. When they noticed it, they merely muttered that I wrote funny, which I knew was not even a backhanded compliment, or said bluntly that it was the wrong way to write, which stung me worse than a nettle. I soothed my injured pride by thinking of myself as a 'clutey' and different from the other pupils in the class, and maybe, in the whole school. But sometimes, I wished I could write with my right hand, like everyone else, never mind touching my nose with my tongue.

In those years, some people believed that using your left hand instead of your right was a bad habit, like biting your nails, or worse, and that it could be cured only by tying the addict's left hand behind his back when he wrote. But you would hear also stories about a certain wee clutey called Sammy, who developed a bad case of nerves from that very cure. Mammy never tried to cure me of the habit, and so I paid little attention to these stories, until the moment I was to be enrolled in Junior Infants. Then the possibility of being tortured and suffering wee Sammy's fate occurred to me.

The Headmistress was seated behind a desk. She looked older than Mammy, but not as old as my Grandma. She looked rich, her hair piled on top of her head and a long string of beads dangling from her neck down the front of a shimmering dark brown dress.

Mammy held me firmly by the hand when she presented me. She gave the headmistress my birth certificate, repeated my name and birth date, and added, after a brief pause, as if she was unsure that this was the proper moment to mention it:

'He's left-handed. Will he be made to write with his other hand?'
She raised my left hand as she said this, as if to show that it had four normal fingers and a thumb where it should be, all clean, and none warty.

'Was he always left-handed?' the Headmistress asked.

'Yis,' said Mammy. 'He's always held his spoon in his left hand.'
I wanted her to add that I threw stones with my left hand, and kicked a wee ball with my left foot, as if she needed additional evidence for my abnormality, but she didn't, and it wasn't necessary anyway.

'Well, Mrs Morrison,' the Headmistress said, 'if William is naturally left-handed, he will not be forced to write with his right hand.'

'That's a relief,' Mammy said, and went on. 'When I was a chile at school, all children were made to write with their right hands.'

The Headmistress looked up from whatever she was writing, and, as if she had been slightly offended by Mammy's remark, said firmly:

'We have stopped doing that at Everton, Mrs Morrison, because we know it is harmful to left-handed children.'

Her gaze passed from Mammy to me, and I took her to mean, 'We won't torment you, William.' I was relieved too, more than Mammy, for it would have been me who would have been tortured. The Headmistress added that I would be placed in Senior Infants, which she taught, but I had enough sense to know that the promotion had nothing to do with my lefthandedness. She kept her word, and I was saved from wee Sammy's fate.

Sandy and I walked to school every day, except the days he was sick, which seemed to be often. We seldom played together on the street because Sandy's mother liked to keep him indoors after he returned from school, or let him play only in his back garden. We never played in each other's house, and when I asked my mother why it was that Sandy couldn't come out to play, she said something I couldn't understand about Sandy's health, and his Mammy's worry, and I put the matter out of my mind. Anyway, I had a little brother and sister to play with, and a baby sister, who had appeared unaccountably one January day beside Mammy in our big bed upstairs, while I was staying at the house next door because Mammy was sick.

The war began, and then Christmas came, and Father Christmas brought me all the way from the North Pole a Canadian Mountie set: a cloth hat with a wide brim for a small head; a Sam Browne belt for a small body; a holster; a revolver for a small hand; and a set of spurs which could be strapped to the heels of my shoes. But no horse.

On Christmas morning, in full uniform and dauntingly armed with a full roll of caps in my revolver, and a spare roll in my pocket, I marched down the street looking for mad dogs and mangy cats and desperadoes, but found none. Anyway, it was hard to maintain law and order when your spurs kept slipping off the heels of your shoes. On my way back to barracks I ran into Sandy. He was lounging under a sombrero at his garden gate, a six-shooter at his hip, and a sheriff's star pinned to his jersey. Because of the shortage of bad guys to apprehend or shoot should they resist arrest, we shot each other several times, then teamed up and fired at invisible foes in the privet hedges of his garden, in innocence of the massacre that had already begun far away, and unsuspecting of a cruel day that lay in wait close at hand.

It was in late February or early March, when the weather is fitful, one day promising spring only to withdraw the gift with a wintry cold hand on the following day, that Sandy fell sick again. One or two days later, I came downstairs for breakfast.

'Sandy goin' t'school th'day?' I asked Mammy.

She shook her head. As she set porridge before me, I saw tears in her eyes.

'Sandy won't be goin' to school anymore,' she said. 'He died durin' th' night.'

I must have looked perplexed.

'Pneumonia,' she added in a low voice like a mutter.

Although I could scarcely pronounce the word, it lodged itself in my vocabulary among the words I already feared, like "drowning" and "suffocating".

Mammy said that the Ruddocks were heartbroken, but I had no idea what grief was. When I asked where Sandy was now, Mammy said, 'Heaven.' All I knew about heaven was that it was a good place to be, for there you never fell sick again, nor wakened in the darkness, because it was never dark.

Yet as I walked that damp morning along our familiar route to Everton, up Glenbryn Drive, down the gravelly Ardoyne Road, where on one side hawthorn and blackberry bushes grew beneath the bare branches of chestnut and sycamore trees, and on the other a greensward ran wild, I felt sorry for Sandy. It was as if he had been cheated by a bigger boy at school, and nobody put it right. And I missed him in a way I hadn't felt before on my solitary walks to school when he was sick.

In the days after Sandy's death, when my schoolbag tipped sideways across my back – which it did often now, because a reader, jotter and a pencil case had usurped the grey slate and stylo – it would occur to me to ask Mammy what had happened to Sandy's schoolbag, but I never did. Nor did I ever again try to touch the tip of my nose with my tongue.

Shortly afterwards, because I had no one to go to school with, I began to run to school. I fell into the habit of getting out of bed late, and leaving myself barely five minutes between setting foot on the street and arriving at school before the last vigorous summons of the school bell had fallen silent. Sometimes, the school door had shut behind the last pupil, when, out of breath, and my schoolbag swinging from the crook of my arm, I reached the school playground. But most often, I was on time.

My leather school bag grew heavier with all sorts of books and colours of penholders and sizes of nibs, as I progressed from Senior Infants to First

Standard and beyond, to Seventh Standard, the last of my school years. For I never did get a new one, like Sandy's bright soft leather bag, with its shiny buckles which, it seemed, he took with him to Heaven. Nor another discarded one. Nor did I have the broken shoulder strap mended.

Throughout the years of the war, leather was scarce, and school bags were made from a composite of cloth and cardboard. They did not endure for long the inclement weather that seemed to be our normal climate, nor withstand the abuse boys gave them. I became attached to my old bag. It had outlasted the war. It was robust: I could fling it on the playground for a goal post for our games of football, and not worry about louts tramping over it; I could whirl it around my body to keep aggressors and mad dogs at bay; I could use it as a shield against stones in a street fight. And always, it kept my books dry.

And, without fuss, year by year I continued to write with my left hand.

Chapter 3

BEYOND THE BEYOND

ON A mild spring evening of 1941, a few German bombers appeared unexpectedly over the city of Belfast. Within a few nights they reappeared in force, and in the hours that followed, Belfast sustained the heaviest single air raid during World War II on any city in the United Kingdom, except London. Bombs fell at the rate of one each minute. Two and a half weeks later they returned to fire bomb the city. Throughout the raids, children all over the city crouched under tables and stairways and huddled on the cement floors of air raid shelters.

EASTER TUESDAY, APRIL 15th 1941
Sometime between 11.00 pm and midnight

For months people said it wouldn't happen, and some even said it couldn't. I can still hear them, the women behind Mammy in the queue at the Co-op where we get dried eggs and flour and margarine with our ration coupons. They were quite sure about it for their men said so:

'My man says them Jerry planes 'ill nivir reach Belfast. Th'ack-acks wud git thim before they gat beyon' Isle a Man,' said one.

'Them that says we cud be bombed is only tryin' to put the wind up ye,' said another.

Heads nodded in agreement.

Well, I have the blinkin' wind up me now, with German bombers right over my head dropping bombs, and me stretched out on a mattress beside my wee brother and sisters, under the kitchen table Daddy has pushed against the wall below the window that looks out on the street. He told us to lie down on the mattress, keep our heads down, be good childer, mind our Mammy, and he'll be back in a while. Then he kissed Mammy and

21

left. He's a St John Ambulance man and when the sirens go he has to go to his first aid station with his white bag of splints and bandages over one shoulder and his gas mask over the other and his tin hat on in case shrapnel hits him.

You can hear lightning crackling, except there's no storm. Some bombs sound like the big front doors of our church slamming shut on a windy Sunday, the echo bouncing around the gallery where we sit. They're the ones that give me the willies for they must be near our house, even though Mammy says they're not. If you listen hard you can hear the ack-ack guns at Cave Hill firing, making a sound like the Lambeg drums Orangemen play around the Twelfth. It was the guns broke the quiet after the sirens had stopped a while ago.

I was sleeping when I heard Mammy's voice calling my name, and I began swimming, slowly, for I can't really swim, through mirk toward a wee light far away. Again she called, soft like, more than a whisper but not a shout, and this time I opened my eyes to see her beside the bed, shaking me with one hand and holding up a candlestick in the other:

'Wake up. Will. Norman, Mavis, Elsie, git up. Get on ye. Just put yer jerseys over yer pajamas and yer socks on. Quickly nigh.'

Half awake, we pushed back the blankets of the big bed we slept in, and rolled off it. I was shivering, not because I was afraid but because I was standing on cold oilcloth while I pulled on my jerseys and socks. Banshees were wailing on windy sills up and down our street. So it seemed. Mammy handed me the candle, and I led the way down the stairs to the kitchen, Mavis who's four and Norman who's six and a half, behind me, and Mammy carrying my baby sister, Elsie. I'll be eight years old in five weeks and five days. We shivered in front of the dead fire grate. Then the sirens stopped, and all was quiet, except for the wooden tick-tock of the big mantelpiece clock. At first, we thought it was another false alarm like other nights last week. Then ack-acks started up, and within a minute you could hear the thuds of somebody dropping trammy peevers one at a time into a huge empty rain barrel. That's what the explosions sounded like, and that's when I had the heebie-jeebies on top of my shivering.

The blinkin' Blitz was here. No doubt this time. But nobody whinged, for Mammy said the bombs were falling far away. We sorted ourselves on the mattress and Mammy threw a blanket over us.

Now that I'm used to the racket outside and not shivering anymore I wish Mammy would let me go out in the street for a wee minute to see the Heinkels and Dorniers. I've seen silhouettes of German airplanes in comics, and so I'd be able to recognise them. But maybe they're too high up to see. At least, you'd hear them. I can hear nothing under this blinkin' table but bombs going off far away.

In daytime, when an airplane flies overhead people look up, listen to the drone, and then somebody says, 'It's one of ours.' German planes have a different sound from ours. I wonder if people really know or do they wait for it to drop a blinkin' bomb, and if it doesn't, then say its ours? I might get an airplane kit for my birthday. Bombers are easier to carve than fighters because they're bigger. And Dorniers carry lots of bombs. Ernie Baker says that if you look up to the sky at night, the bomb-aimers can see your white face. Ha! Ha! That's going beyond the beyond, as my Grandma in Ligoniel would say.

Grandma and Granda Morrison always give us big chocolate eggs for Easter and yesterday we threw them up to hit the ceiling and then let them smash on the floor. The bits of chocolate shell scattered over the oilcloth. Mammy would barge us if we did that at any other time, but she doesn't mind at Easter.

If a bomb hits us, this table will stop the ceiling falling on us even though it'll make a mess of the table top. Touch wood. It feels rough, not like the top Mammy polishes every Friday. You're not allowed to put your electric light on after the sirens go, but you can light a candle. It's not as bright but it makes better animal heads on the wall. And you shouldn't raise your windy blind at night even if you only have candlelight, because there's a "Blackout".

The day the Blackout started Mammy was on our door stoop gossiping with Mrs Hynes on her door stoop, when the paperboy brought *The Belfast Telegraph*, the 'Tele', we call it. Black letters as thick as your finger across the top of the front page: 'BLACKOUT'. I couldn't stop a smile, the sort you have when you hear you might be going to the seaside, because a BLACKOUT meant that there might be a Blitz or air raids on Belfast. Mammy called the news to Mrs Hynes and the two of them wondered if there was any call for it.

Before the blackout, if you were on the Horseshoe Road beyond the top of our street at night you could look over Belfast and see hundreds of street lights below you and the sky glimmering above. Now it's like the sea at night, even when the moon shines. The coloured lights outside the big shops and Grand Hotel on Royal Avenue downtown have gone, and the lights that used to flit and wink outside the Opera House have disappeared, and weren't even back for the pantomime there last Christmas.

Mammy says we should try to sleep, but I don't want to sleep; I want to listen for bombs. What a blinkin' racket! Somebody's hammering with our door knocker and shouting, 'Missus Marsen, Missus Marsen.' Mammy says; 'In God's name. That's Mrs Sterrit. An' in th' middle of an air raid,' and lets her in. She has roly-poly Bobby and his wee brother and sister with her. Her husband's in the army, in the desert, I think, or in England. She's in a state. She says that she was on her way home with the childer from visiting her mammy when the sirens went and when she reached her house, two doors above us, she couldn't find her house key. She should've hung it on a piece of cord behind the letterbox, like we do. There she was, out on the street with her weans and bombs already falling. We scrunch up on the mattress to make room for three more until I'm half sitting, up against the blinkin' wall.

Mammy makes Mrs Sterrit a cup of tea, then raps a poker on the wall between us and the Hynes and on the one between us and the McNallys. They both rap back, so they must be all right. Mr Hynes is in the army and Mr McNally is a merchant seaman, and both are away. The Hynes have three and the McNallys five. I wonder if they're under their table too. Herbie Hynes is my age, and my friend, and he has a sister a year older and a big brother. Wee Mary McNally plays with my sister Mavis, and sometimes Sean plays with Herbie and me even though they're Roman Catholics.

We've been under this table a long time and the Blitz hasn't stopped.

Daddy hasn't come back yet. Maybe we should be in the air-raid shelter down the street. They have room enough for thirty people or so. Mammy said when they built them, 'You'd be safer in yur own house than in them concrete coffins.' That's why we lie under a table. "Morrison shelter", it's called, not after us but after some bigwig in England. He said that if you don't have an Anderson shelter in your back garden, then shove a table beneath a window and get under it.

I hate walking past the blinkin' air-raid shelters in the dark. They don't have doors, only doorways, and are pitch black inside. Fellas and girls doll in there at night. They're smelly places because drunk men piss and boke in them. Still, if you're out on a dark night and have to pee you can juke into a shelter. If you're not too scared.

On moonless nights outside you can't see your hand in front of your face. You need cats' eyes to walk along the street without slipping on spit or tramping on dog keek that sticks to your instep and gets around the lining of your uppers. And it takes a lion's nerves to keep you from wetting your trousers when you hear footsteps behind you, especially if you take a short cut home from the Crumlin Road through the streets where the Catholics live.

There goes the big mantelpiece clock again, whirring itself up as if about to cough up catarrh, so that the hammer will strike the chime loud enough for the deaf to hear. Twelve chimes, banging round the kitchen walls. I get to stay up this late only on the Eleventh night when we light bonefires for the Twelfth. I'm not even a junior Orangeman – Daddy wouldn't let me join it, and he's not an Orangeman either – but I like the bonefires.

Maybe I should ask Mammy to blow out the candle so that I can peek out behind the window blind. She let me look out of our bedroom window when the docks were being bombed a week ago. You could see flashes in the distance. The sirens had wakened us but only Daddy, Mammy and me got out of bed, and Mammy didn't even bother to light a candle.

This raid's bigger, and Mammy might barge me for asking. It might upset Mrs Sterrit too. I wonder if she has really lost her house key?

You can hear an ARP whistle outside. Like a football referee's. Maybe an ARP man has caught somebody shining a light. People say that the IRA in the Catholic 'Bone' below our street and up the Falls Road light bonefires and shine torches into the sky to guide any Germans bombers that turn up. If they do, it's blinkin' daft. Planes drop bombs on lights. The peelers and IRA have fired on each other up in Estorial Park in the Ardoyne.

Used to be you only had to look out for blinkin' peelers, but now you have to watch for the ARP, the 'Air Raid Precautions' wardens. But only at night. They can't arrest you, but have authority to shout at you, 'PUT OUT THAT LIGHT!' They go round the streets at night to make sure nobody's windy blind leaks light, and gulder at anyone who lights a cigarette in the dark or waves its red tip about. You should step into an air-raid shelter to light your feg, and hold it in toward the palm of your hand, like Daddy does. Air raid wardens give you the jitters sometimes. When people hear that they are doing their rounds in their street, they run outside to see if their windy blinds let out a crack of light, for they say it only takes a crack to give away the position of your house to enemy bombers. Anybody over sixteen can join the ARP, Daddy said. You get a tin hat with the letters ARP on it, an arm band with ARP on it, and a gas-mask you carry in a haversack slung from your shoulder, like a soldier's. Not like mine, in a cardboard box with a cord sling.

There's supposed to be a full moon tonight, last night's 'Tele' said. It was cloudy today, I mean yesterday, but the sky cleared a bit by tea time. Bomber pilots like moonlight, but you'd think it would help ack-ack gunners more. Nobody can black out the moon. You can't gulder at God, 'Put out that light!' You have to depend on clouds to do it. But clouds come and go as they please.

I can hear a gun wumping near us now. Mammy says they must have put an ack-ack near the flax mill behind Jamaica Street. That's at the bottom end of our street, but no matter; an ack-ack gun down there will keep the bombs away from us. Touch wood twice.

Sometime between 1.00 am and 2.00 am

The noise of bombs is getting louder. Ohh! That one was loud. Like Finn McCool putting his boot to our backyard door.

'Mammy, was that near us?'

'Whisht. Yer alright when ye can hear thim.'

I'm still shaking, I don't mind telling you. A bomb's fin spins as it falls and makes it whistle and I'm sure I heard its whistle. That was blinkin' near us, no matter what Mammy says.

Why is Daddy not back yet?

Everything is quiet now. Too quiet. Something's wrong.

'Mammy.'

'Lie down, Will. What is it nigh?'

'Th' gun down Jamaica Street's stopped firin'.'

I listen for its wump. Nothing. I'm thinking about that explosion we just heard. I know I'm right. She says they're resting, they've been firing all night. Norman is sitting up too, his eyes wide open. We listen hard. No guns are firing, but the air raid isn't over. The quiet lasts only a minute or so. Bombs are going off all over again, far and near, and my heart's thumping the way it does when I'm belting down the street, trying to catch a blinkin' runaway hoop with my cleak.

Later

Someone is at the door. A quiet voice; 'Youse all right here?' It's Daddy. After a word to Mrs Sterrit, he drops his ambulance bag and gas mask beside the coal hole door, and he and Mammy go into the scullery.

I carry my gas mask to school every day, slung from my shoulder on a piece of cord. It makes you feel you're doing 'your bit in the war', as people say. Like the Home Guard, only you're not allowed to have a rifle unless you're sixteen. I wonder if the Germans will drop mustard gas, like they did in the Great War my Uncle Joe was in? I hate mustard. Sometimes Mammy puts it in the hot bath if we get soaked walking in the rain. So that we won't get pneumonia.

At school we have these blinkin' gas mask inspections. Nobody really likes them even though you get out of school for a while. You're marched into the playground and told to get ready. So, you take your mask out of its box, wrestle your face into it, pull the straps hard behind your head until the rubber is tight against your face, and the glass window is straight to see out of. The canister you breath in and out of covers your nose and chin, making you look for all the world as if you have some class of pig's snout. If it leaks, you're done for, somebody said, but nobody ever knew of anybody croaking at an inspection.

Then you're marched in groups into a caravan and sit on benches. A warden in a gas mask with two big round glass windows and a tube like a baby elephant's trunk hanging from his nose and mouth into a bag on his chest, comes in and shuts the door behind him. They fill the caravan with tear gas, and we breathe through our snouts like pigs snoring. Once I tried not breathing in. After a minute my eyes must have bulged, for the blinkin' warden shouted at me and gave me a shake so that I breathed hard out through the mask, and sucked in gobs of tear gas, making my eyes run like rivers. If you get scared, the warden doesn't let you out. He checks your mask for leaks. I never know what he says for his voice comes from far away. But it doesn't matter. If you're not gasping and rolling about in agony, and able to nod to him he seems to be satisfied. It's always a relief to get out of the caravan and the gas mask off. Everybody has tears in his eyes, so you can't tell who has been scared but has held it in, like wanting to do a flood when your bladder's bursting and your willy has a drip at its tip.

I'm usually like that when I'm excited about going somewhere – 'Mister Will always has't go to th' lavatry when we're goin' out th' door,' Mammy says. When I'm scared at a murder picture, I always want to do a flood. I could do it right there under the seat, but I don't. Not like some people at the pictures. Sometimes you have to lift your feet to let the flood from somebody in the rows behind you run under you. But I haven't wanted to go all night, not even when that blinkin' bomb fell close – no matter what Mammy says.

The explosions are not so loud nor so often now. Daddy's gone again; he only stayed a minute or two. Mammy never says anything about Daddy leaving, but I'm sure she wishes he would stay. Mrs Sterrit is sitting up on the sofa with the baby in her arms. Elsie is sleeping, but Mavis and Norman are awake. So are the Sterrits. We don't talk. It's nearly four o'clock in the morning, so we've been lying here for five hours.

About 4.00 am

There hasn't been an explosion for a while, and Mammy says she thinks it's over. So she tells us to listen for the 'All Clear'. We all sit up, all ears, and eyes, for that matter, because they look big and shine in the candlelight. Except for the bells of fire engines afar off, all is quiet, like in school when Miss Hutchinson wants to hear a pin drop. A funny quiet.

There it is. The 'All Clear'. A low growl rising to a high drone like a suffering bagpipe. On and on it whines, and you can hear the doors of houses banging, then voices in the street. Mammy opens the door and we trek after her into the front garden. The air smells of burnt rags. I feel whacked, I don't mind telling you, but at the same time, like I've got a day off school. You feel as light as a feather when the 'All Clear' drones.

We weren't hit, and it'll be daylight soon.

INTERLUDE
Wednesday, April 16th
Morning

You should see the sky: a smoky, dirty yellow, as if it's sick.

The water has been turned off; the firemen need it to put out the fires, though somebody said the mains were wrecked by bombs, and if it isn't turned on tomorrow we will have to go to Grandma Morrison's for some. She lives in Ligoniel and has spring water. But it takes ages to walk there and home again with a bucket of water. Mammy has saved some in the kettle and pots; she always does that when the sirens go. For porridge and tea. But there's no water to wash your face. And the gas has been cut off too; so, we'll have to boil the kettle on the grate. We don't know if the Gas Works has been hit. It's a good job we have coal.

Daddy has come home for a wee while. He said that North Belfast – that's us – got most bombs. Whole streets flattened by parachute mines. They are worse than the big bombs. They float down and lie on the ground, and then in a minute or in an hour or so, go off. One fell beside an air-raid shelter full of people in Percy Street, Daddy said. Everybody was killed. Mammy only shook her head. Daddy said no other shelter was hit, as far as he knew. I think direct hits will kill you no matter where you are, except deep underground. Like in the London tubes.

Granda Porter and Uncle John are coming to stay with us. They live in the Bone, down Oldpark Road, which was badly hit. I have to watch for them while I'm playing on the street with my chums. We're not really playing; just talking about where the bombs hit and how many people have been killed.

Afternoon

Herbie is here to see if I'm ready to go and see the bomb damage and to look for shrapnel. Bobbie, his big brother, is going with us, and so we'll be safe.

'An' we won't pick up any fountain pens,' I tell Mammy.

'What?' she says.

'Everybody says th' Germans dropped fountain pens that'll explode when ye pick them up.'

Mammy seems to think that's funny and I tell her it's true, Nazis do that.

'Where ye goin' so as I'll know where ye are?' she asks.

'Ardoyne, and then down Crumlin to Agnes Street.'

'You be careful, nigh, an' don't you go near Percy Street.'

She always says 'you' when she's warning me. Percy Street is near the Shankill end of Agnes Street, where we are going.

I can go now because Granda Porter and Uncle John are here. I saw them coming up the street; Granda with a wee attaché case in one hand and a bird cage covered with a cloth in the other, and his face boggin' with soot and white dust. He's a wee man, and he looked funny beside my uncle John who is tall and hadn't a speck of soot on him. When Mammy saw him she laughed, 'In God's name what happened t' you?' and we all laughed too.

Well, during the raid he was sitting in his wee kitchen by the range when a bomb blast blew soot down the chimney and shook the plaster off the ceiling. Uncle John was standing at the front door at that time. They were lucky. Whole streets were wiped out in the Bone. Nine in one house in Ballynure Street behind him were killed. I told him that we had eleven people in our house, counting the Sterrits' baby. Granda and Uncle John are going to stay with us until it is safe to go back to their house. So is Granda's canary. The blinkin' bird sang in its cage while we talked. Never stopped.

Tea-time

I'm whacked. I've been all over the Crumlin and Shankill Roads. The roof of Ardoyne Tram Depot is on top of the trams. The firemen are still trying to put out Ewart's mill. All that stuff they spin and weave there must burn for hours. You should see the mountains of bricks and slates and broken wood down streets that were hit, walls with no roofs, roofs half torn off, and whole fronts and sides ripped off houses so that you can see tables and chairs in the kitchens and beds in bedrooms, but all in a mess with bits of curtains and plaster. Some houses still smoke. We saw air-raid wardens and soldiers pulling away bricks and bits of plaster lath and furniture from rubble, and Army lorries alongside. To take away bodies, I heard a woman say. The peelers had barriers up around Percy Street. You keep thinking of the people killed there even if you don't know them, and then you think you might have been too because you don't know where the bombs will hit.

But here's a quare geg, and we had a great laugh when we saw it. Our blinkin' school got hit. Yes. A parachute mine fell into the field next door and wrecked one side of it, and left a huge crater almost as deep as the quarry up the Horseshoe Road. Herbie and Bobby weren't half as excited as me. I was fair jumping. 'Lucky dog, Marrisen,' they said. They thought then we should go over to the Oldpark Road to see if their school got hit. Anyway, we're leaving the 'Bone' until tomorrow.

I found two wee bits of jaggy bomb shrapnel. They feel queer; one side smooth and shiny, the other rough with tiny ridges. I'm going to Cave Hill tomorrow. Somebody said that the Messerschmitts planes with the bombers had machine-gunned the streets there, trying to hit the ack-ack guns, so I might find some dunted bullets. I didn't see any fountain pens lying around.

Thursday, April 17th
Evening: *Tea-time*

Our 'Tele' has pages on the Blitz; stories and pictures. And miles of death notices in the 'Births, Marriages, Deaths' page. York Street Spinning Mill, six stories high, was blown apart and half of it fell on rows of houses beside it, flattening over forty of them with people inside. They're using St George's Market and Falls Road Swimming Baths as morgues because the hospitals have nowhere to put the bodies. Many of the dead haven't been claimed, it says, so there's going to be a mass grave for them. Whole families must have been killed. It's all very sad, being dead and nobody missing you.

Earlier today we went up to swanky parts of Carr's Glen and the North Circular Road near Cave Hill, and then down to the Bone. The sky was a brilliant blue, as if it had never been dirtied. The wreckage of the big houses lay scattered about the big sunny gardens. Down the Oldpark Road long hills of rubble stretched where there used to be rows of houses. Half of the Bone is gone. Herbie was disappointed that Finiston School was still standing.

We couldn't find any dunted bullets.

Monday, April 21st
Evening

It's hard to sleep after being back at school, if you know what I mean. I didn't think we'd have to go since it was half blown up, but our classroom was in one piece. Not everybody was present. Anyway, our teacher, Miss Hutchinson, told Bertie Bigger to fill up the inkwells in all the desks, and she fistled with the roll book after she called our names. Maybe the absent ones didn't know school had started again.

Everybody's wondering if the Germans will be back. Nobody's saying they won't, for we know now we are not at the blinkin' back of beyond. The evenings are longer and I don't go to bed as early, but sometimes I have hardly shut my eyes before the Alert sounds. We get up, and sit on the sofa downstairs until Daddy comes back from the First Aid Station. We don't even bother getting under the table. Mammy gets annoyed. 'It's goin' a bit too far, every night. You'd think th' Civil Defence had a bit of sense,' she says.

People are starting to run for the hills at the first squeak of the siren. A lot come up our street because it's the way to the fields and ditches off the Horseshoe Road. The first night after the air raid the sirens went off, and while we're sitting on the sofa waiting to see what we should do next, we hear this queer sound in the street outside; murmuring, shuffling, running. Mammy blows out the candle in case a blinkin' warden might gulder at us, opens the front door, and we all go into our garden. It's dark, but a moon sails in and out of clouds.

Our street is thick with people rushing up to the fields. Old women arm-in-arm with younger ones shuffle by, and you can see strings of beads hanging from their fingers. Big girls trail wee ones by the hand. Old fellas push themselves headlong with their walking sticks. Women push prams, their weans hanging to the handles and sides and running as fast as their wee legs will let them, and staying as best they can out of the way of the wheels and their mothers' feet. Some prams are loaded like a ragman's cart and wobble, creak and screech for want of oil. One passing close to me has a mantelpiece clock lying at the baby's feet. And now and again you can hear a woman telling a whinging child to shut up or the Germans would hear it. The air hums, rising and falling: 'Hail Mary, Mother of God…' 'full of grace…' 'pray for us sinners'. Catholics from the streets below us, Mammy says, and the Bone, God help them. They were badly hit in the big raid.

Thursday, May 1st
Morning

With the sirens going every night everybody is saying there's going to be another big raid. Some people on our street have dug wee trenches up in the fields beside the Dig for Victory potato plots. Nobody wants to go into air-raid shelters. Last Saturday we dug our trench, Herbie, Bobby and me. We carried the sods and good dark soil in my four-wheel guider for our back gardens. You can stand up in the trench but it's narrow. I can't see it holding both our families, but we dug 'til our hands were sore from the shovels. We put an old piece of oilcloth on the bottom. I hope it doesn't rain for we'll have to sit in it.

Air raid wardens came to our school on Monday and we were marched into the playground. They showed us dummy incendiary bombs and told us they are worse than high explosives because they spread fire. A big man with an ARP arm band shouted at us, 'Stairs is safest if blast wrecks your house.' That's true. In some bombed out houses I saw, the stairs were the only thing standing. But then he went on; 'But not if it catches fire. So, don't take cover under yer stairs; it's th' worst place if an incenary hits yer house. For stairs are tinder dry, an' burn like matches.' I know that if you get a direct hit you're goners, and you wouldn't even know it, but if an incendiary bomb comes through your roof, you might be able to put it out or get out before your house goes up in a blaze. Throw a sandbag on it, the ARP man told us. You should keep a sandbag and a bucket of water handy, he said. Next, he showed us how to work a stirrup pump. You put the pump in a bucket of water and you pump with one hand and aim the wee hose with the other. It took two of us, Bertie Biggar and me, to do it. I tried to lift a sandbag to throw it on a dummy incendiary, but the bag didn't budge and I nearly fell over it.

After school I told Mammy we needed a sandbag and a stirrup pump. And should have a bucket of water always standing beside the chimney. 'An' how are ye Burke,' she said, as she usually does when I tell her about things we should have. 'Where'll we git money for a stirrup pump? An' where're ye goin't'git a sandbeg from?' Well, I thought we could ask the ARP for a sandbag, or pinch one from somewhere, but from her tone of voice I knew there was no use arguing about it. So, I didn't say anything about the stairs either.

Monday, May 4th
About 1.00 am

Mammy's voice sounds different from other nights; sharp and quick, like when she's barging us, only she's not. 'Come on, all of youse. Get up. Quick. Get on ye. Just pull yer trousers and jersey over yer pajamas. Put yer shoes on.' She puts Mavis and Elsie into their siren suits, and hands Norman and me our overcoats.

'Why, Mammy?'

'In case we have t' run.'

Beyond the banshee wail of the sirens, guns are already firing.

When we get downstairs Granda Porter and Uncle John are already up because they sleep in the wee room off the scullery. Daddy is putting on his St John's uniform. There's no mattress on the floor.

Mammy sets the candle on the mantelpiece, and shadows twitch and shift shapes on the walls. Outside, the street murmurs and creaks again. I hear wee children cry, and open the front door. Down the street a warden gulders at somebody. Mammy shouts at me:

'Will, get you in here.'

'He's not shouting at us. Somebody's lit a feg. Aren't we going up th' fields?'

'No, get inside.'

We wait to be told what to do next. Then, Daddy tells Mammy:

'Get them childer int'a th' coal hole.'

The cupboard under the stairs. We sometimes keep coal there to save us having to go out to the yard on a wild wet night. And it keeps the coal dry. I am about to blurt out what the air raid warden told us last week in school but I might get barged for being contrary, so I say nothing and do as I'm told. You have to put your head down in the coal hole or you'll hit the blinkin' stairs above you. It's boggin' with coal dust and there's no room to lie down, but Mammy has put newspapers on the floor. We crawl in, hunker our knees to our chins. Granda Porter and Mammy squeeze in near the door. She has the big torch I got in my Christmas stocking; it takes three batteries. We use it sometimes in the yard at night to get a shovel of coal. The coal hole door is ajar and I can hear Uncle John moving about the kitchen.

The guns and explosions have already started, just like on Easter Tuesday. I don't want to scare Norman and Mavis, but I feel queer about this. Why are we sitting under these blinkin' stairs? I can't hold the question back any longer.

'Why don't we go up th' fields, Mammy? T' our wee trench?'

'Shush,' she says. 'We're all right here.'

Not if a blinkin' incendiary hits the house.

It's awfully quiet in here. You can't even hear what's going on in the street outside. Our eyes shine in the torch light, and we all stare as if something bad is going to happen. Like at school when Miss Hutchinson is barging the class for something wrong and you're waiting for her to call your name and send you to Old Hutchy, the headmaster, even though you didn't do anything wrong.

The pupils of my wee sisters' eyes look like blots of ink you drop from an overfull nib. They stare at Mammy. Are they scared too? Is Mammy? I don't mind telling you that's how I feel stuck under these stairs. My legs are getting stiff from not being able to stretch them. And my bum's numb from being flattened on the floor. If a blinkin' incendiary comes down the chimney I won't be able to move fast enough even to pish on it, not that that would do any good, if the ARP man at school is right.

We've been hit! We've been hit, Mammy!

But the words stay in my mind for my ears are dinning with the explosion, and somewhere in the dinning I hear glass splinter and something slam against the sideboard and something else thump on the stairs over us, all at once. Mammy cries out, 'Dear God,' and switches off the torch. I can't see anybody's face in the coal hole. We don't move for a minute. Then Mammy shouts:

'Youse all right Billy?'

'I'm awright. Th' blast threw me up th' stairs. Get th' childer out ave there.'

I thought Daddy had gone to his station. He was standing at the front door the whole time. Mammy calls us, and we creep out from the coal hole, head down, waddling like ducks. Daddy's in his shirtsleeves, his braces hanging down the sides of his black trousers. There's glass everywhere. I feel tingly, the sort you get in your willy when you're about to do a dare, like jumping off the roof of an air-raid shelter. Daddy tells Mammy:

'Better take them childer up th' fields, Mabel.'

Mammy starts fussing at Norman and me:

'Come on, youse. Button yer coats.'

I'm fiddling with my buttons when a man hammers on our front door.

'Billy Marrison. Billy Marrison. There's a casulty across th' street.'

Daddy grabs his white bag and rushes out the front door. I start to follow him, just to get outside, but Mammy stops me:

'Here you. Take Norman by th' han' and get up inta th' fields. Yer Granda an' Uncle John are goan with ye. Come on, nigh.'

Uncle John picks up Elsie, takes Mavis by the hand and leads the way, with Norman and me hand in hand close behind, out of the house and on to the street. Mammy and Granda follow us.

It's like daylight, but it's only about two in the morning. The air stinks of a dying bonefire on a rainy night. But it's not raining. ARP men are running toward the wrecked houses across the street. I can't see Daddy. We half-run up the street, Uncle John trailing Mavis, me trailing Norman because their legs are shorter than ours, to the fields where our trench is. Every now and again when I look behind me, I see more of the sky burning. All over the fields people are sitting or lying about in the ditches. We come to a space in a ditch. It's not our trench, but Mammy says;

'Here. This'll do.'

'But Mammy, we dug a trench. Shine yer torch, it must be near.'

'We haven't time to look for yer trench. Just, git inta th' ditch.'

The ditch is dry, but not deep. I wonder if somebody is already in our trench, sitting on our oilcloth. Mammy orders us, 'Lie down, nigh, and don't look up.' Does *she* think the Germans will see our blinkin' faces? People have been saying that the planes are machine-gunning the streets out of the city. But we hear no machine-guns, and after a while we stand up to look around. I can hardly believe my eyes.

The fields here are high enough that on a clear day you can look across the city and see in the far distance Slieve Donard, the highest mountain in Ireland. It's lost now in the darkness beyond the burning city. And we have a grandstand view of the fires.

Above us, the sky is red and orange with fire, and white-yellow-black smoke spirals upwards in columns into that terrible light. Sparks rise high above rooftops and fall down again like red and golden rain. Just a stone's throw beyond the bottom of our street, maybe Deerpark Road, some houses are burning, and the factory behind Jamaica Street shoots great balls of sparks and smoke into the sky. Mammy points out a fierce fire on the Oldpark Road opposite the Park picture house – that's where we go to Saturday matinee. 'St Silas's Church,' she says. That's where she and Daddy were married. Its spire is burning like a Roman candle above the blazing roof.

The queer thing is that although the sky is bright, the fields around us and at our feet are dark. You can't clearly see a blade of grass. I can't see any bombers and fighters either, nor hear them, but they must still be up there because I see explosions far away.

Somebody in the field near us must have lit a cigarette or a switched on a torch for a man's hard voice gulders 'PUT OUT THAT LIGHT!' and somebody laughs and we join in. But just for a second. Maybe we're all thinking the same thing.

Monday, May 5th
Evening

Last night we didn't get to bed until it was almost the break of day. We sat up the fields until the All Clear went, and came back to the house. It was in one piece but we had to clear bits of plaster and glass off our bed before we got into it. Mammy hung an old sheet over the broken window to keep the draught out.

A row of houses across the street is completely wrecked. Two houses have caved in entirely and only the stairs are still standing. There's a deep hole in a front garden where the bomb buried itself before exploding. Daddy says we're lucky. If the bomb had hit the street instead of going into a front garden the explosion would have completely wrecked our house and others, and the blast might have killed all of us. I ask him if anybody was killed:

'Three houses was empty. They must've went up th' fields. Them in th' end one was shuk up by th' blast.'

'So, who were ye sent for then?'

'A young lad from down th' street. He was passin' an' th' bomb lofted him like a futball intil th' entry.' He points across the street to the side of the row of houses. 'He was kilt by th' blast. He should've gone down on his hans an' knees on th' street when he heard th' bomb comin', let th' blast go under him, but he threw himself flat on th' concrete.'

'How old is he?'

'A lad about fifteen.'

I don't ask what he was doing out on the street when the bomb fell. It bothers me that I can't picture his face because he is from down the street and older than me. But I have learned what to do what a bomb falls near; don't flatten yourself, crouch.

Everybody is talking about the thousands of incendiaries that must have fallen to start the big fires we saw during the night. I go up Deerpark Road with Herbie and over to the Oldpark Road to see what is left of St Silas's Church of Ireland. We pass a house at the corner of Deerpark Road and Alliance Avenue that had been hit by incendiaries. Nothing much is left of it but bricks and bits of smouldering wood and ashes. Not even stairs. In the middle of the rubble a sewing machine, or what was left of it, sits crookedly. The wood around it has burned away and wisps of smoke still drift up from the iron frame and pedal. It reminds me of Mammy pedalling away on hers, sewing the arse back in my trousers. Before all this happened. This Blitz. I wonder about the people who lived in that house. Were they under the stairs or did they get out in time?

Nothing much left either of St Silas's. Four walls and smoke still coming from behind them where the burning roof and spire have fallen in. Across the road, the Park picture house is still standing. All in one piece. Maybe there will be a Saturday matinee.

Evening

We're wondering if we should go to bed at all, but Daddy says he doesn't think the Germans will be back so soon. 'This isn't Lont'n where they git bombed ivery night.' No, we're not London, but still the Germans might be back. After all, everybody once said Belfast was beyond them, and they were wrong.

Epilogue

The Luftwaffe didn't come back. Two months later, Russia had entered the war, and Hitler called off his campaign of systematic bombing of cities in the United Kingdom. In comparison to the mass destruction of cities and civilians in Europe and in the Far East in the later years of the war, and, I might add, of the wars to come, where 'beyond the beyond' became for many human beings an unimaginable horror, the raids on Belfast were not exceptional. And my experience as a child under blitz pales beside the terrible suffering other children endured, and still endure, when death falls from the skies.

During the Easter Tuesday raid on Belfast, the bombers had overshot the industrial targets, and many bombs, particularly high explosive parachute mines designed to penetrate steel and concrete roofs of factories, fell on the densely populated streets of residential environs, such as North Belfast, exacting a heavy toll on civilians: over nine hundred killed and thousands injured. By contrast, despite the fires and fire storms that raged through the city on the night of May 4th, the number killed was much lower, although more than half of these were women and children. This difference may be explained in part by the fact that many people with relatives in the country had already left the city, and those remaining, at the first sound of the Alert, fled their houses for the fields and hills around the city. In the raids, more than half of the city's houses were destroyed or badly damaged. The Luftwaffe did not lose a single plane.

Their luck held for the incendiary raid on May 4th during which they dropped 95,992 incendiaries and 237 tons of high explosives. The only change the authorities made to the city's defences following the Easter Tuesday raid was to shoot 33 animals, including a vulture, at the Belfast Zoo, who were deemed to be a public danger should the zoo be bombed. The list included two raccoons.

In our family, as we were growing up, we rarely discussed the Blitz. It was as though it was just one of those things that come with life. Sometimes we would recall the events I have already narrated in my story, but of my father's deeds as an ambulance man we learned little, and nothing of my mother's fears and feelings, like those of many mothers, I suppose, who 'minded the childer' while their menfolk fought wars and fires and rescued the injured and retrieved the dead. Only once did my father mention his work during the Blitz. Shortly after the last air raid he told us of entering a bomb-damaged house to find a family sitting and lying about their kitchen, dead, and without a mark, let alone a wound, on any of them. Blast from a bomb had sucked the oxygen out of their lungs. Why he told us that story and not others remains a mystery. I suspect it was because we had barely escaped that fate.

Chapter 4

INTO THE UNKNOWN

WHEN THE Government decided to evacuate all the children from Belfast after the third German air raid on the city, I was not pleased. I didn't want to go, even though my instinct warned me that if the bombers returned – and I was sure they would, for they had been repeatedly hammering London – I would be safer deep in the country than hunkered under tinder dry stairs or huddled in an air raid shelter. I liked the countryside, and often walked to Cave Hill and up the Horseshoe Road to Squire's Hill, but I wanted to be able to say, when the war was over, that I had seen all the air raids, and didn't run away.

But whatever I felt or wanted didn't matter; I was only eight years of age and had to do what I was told. And so, with thousands of other children, with my younger brother, sisters and mother, I left the blitzed city.

On the day of the evacuation mother shook us at dawn, for we had to catch an early tram to take us to the railway station, and to her surprise, I swung out of bed as if it was Christmas morning. Most mornings, to her annoyance, I preferred the bliss of sleep to the glories of the day's awakening. But after weeks of having my sleep interrupted by air raid sirens, I could hit the cold oilcloth without a whimper, if I had good reason to do so. Being evacuated might be like being forced to run away from the enemy, but it was also like dipping into a lucky bag; you didn't know what you were going to pull out, but you knew you would get something. And maybe we would be lucky, and be sent to the seaside. This was no morning for indolence.

Within minutes, the house got the days of the week mixed up. It was a weekday, but the house bustled as if it was a churchgoing Sunday. I shouted down the stairs to the kitchen:

'Mammy, what'll we put on?'

'Yer gud clothes,' she shouted back.

'Th' ones we wear on Sunday?'

'What other gud ones do ye have?'

There was a hush as if the house had gone back to sleep. Then another shout shot up the stairs:

'An don't forget t' comb yer hair.'

Dressed in my grey single-breasted suit, white shirt with the starched collar and cuffs, and a tie with diagonal stripes, socks and shoes, I presented myself to the wardrobe mirror. Did James Cagney part his hair on the left side or right? Or down the middle? I settled for left side. After all, I was clutey. I combed until a thin white slightly crooked line stretched from my forehead to the back of my head like a twist of twine. I helped my brother Norman push a similar parting through his sandy hair, and went down stairs.

My mother was vigorously brushing my sister Mavis's sleep-tatted auburn mop, ignoring her mewls. She turned to me:

'Did ye comb yir hair?'

'Yis.'

'Fix yer socks. Is them yer gud socks?'

'Yis.'

'Com'ere. Let me see.'

She examined the darning in the heels of the socks for threats of holes.

'Did ye put elastic garters roun th' tops?'

'I did.'

'Well, straighten them.'

I looked down. The blue bands below my knees were crooked. I did as I was told, and snapped the white elastic to make sure it would hold the socks up. My father enquired whether we had cleaned and shone our shoes the night before. That was the limit.

'Daddy, wur only bein' evacyated; wur nat goin' t'church.'

'I know, but ye nivir know whose yir be'an evacuated to, an' if they see ye wi' dirty shoes they'll think youse come from a dirty house.'

There was something not quite right about this argument, but I said nothing.

We picked up our bowls of porridge in the scullery, and made a space

for ourselves at the table in the kitchen. Because the table sat against the
wall and below the front window to give us more room to pass one another
in the middle of the small kitchen, and in these recent days to shelter us
during the air raids, it could take only three chairs. Being the eldest and
least expected to spill my porridge, I stood. A newspaper lay draped on the
table, held in place with a bottle of milk and a bowl of sugar, and between
reluctant mouthfuls of porridge, I scanned the headlines, which described
the evacuation and looked for predictions about future enemy raids. My
mother broke into my research:

'Eat up, nigh, all of yis, for ye'll git nothin' much the rest of th' day.
An' wipe yir faces with th' face cloth when ye've done. I don't want ye
lukin' like gypsies. An' you, mister Will, stap readin'. Ye eat slow enough
as t'is.'

After toast and hot tea, we wiped our faces at the jaw box in the scullery,
and waited for the word to go. Our mother inspected us:

'Alright. Iverybody been to the lavatry? You, mister Will? I don't want
you waitin' 'til we're out on th' street, an' then as usual, you havin' t'rush
back in t'do a flood.'

'Yis.'

Though it was mid-May, Norman and I belted ourselves into our worsted
overcoats. 'Less of a nuisance worn than carried over yir arms,' Mammy
had said. She set Elsie, the youngest of us at two and a half years old, in her
pushchair:

'Youse all ready? Got yur gas masks?'

'Yis.'

'Sure ye don't have t' do a flood, Mister Will?'

'No.'

'Well, all of ye, out ye go.'

Father lifted the large case, I picked the wee attaché case we had borrowed
from my Granda Porter. Our escape from harm's way had begun. So too,
had our journey into the unknown.

We left the house to recover its equanimity and its appropriate sense
of the quotidian. Norman, Mavis, and I in the vanguard at our mother's

prompting, our gas masks bumping against our hips, my Granda's wee case gripped stiffly in my fist, we marched to rhythm of the pushchair's wheels down the still slumbering street, past the rubble of four houses hit in the last air-raid, past the burnt shells of houses on another, until we reached the tram stop on the Oldpark Road.

It seemed as if in the east the city was again on fire, but it was only the rose and yellow hem of the brightening sky. The weather for the evacuation was going to be glorious, whatever else the day, and the days to come, held in store.

The tram rumbled and clanked its way to the heart of the sorely wounded city, past the blackened skeleton of St Silas's Church and the blasted streets of the Bone where many had died. We called out the streets as the tram passed them: Ballynure Street, Ballycastle Street, Ballymoney Street, a naming whose import we didn't understand, and as it approached Ballymena Street we craned to glimpse the house where I was born and had spent my first four years. It was intact but dishevelled with broken windows like my Granda's house further down the row. It was a wonder that the street had been spared, so great was the devastation around it, streets flattened by bombs. As the tram passed through the junction of Agnes Street and across Carlisle Circus into the downtown, we could see more destruction. It seemed the city had been destroyed except for pockets of houses and buildings that had refused to fall. The terror of the recent nights came back to me, and the excitement. But I was too young to feel the horror of it all.

The Great Northern Railway Station boomed with the hullabaloo of an excursion day. The din met you as you passed between the lofty pillars of its portal and pulled you into its vortex. Overhead, the vault of girders and glass echoed the racket of trains shunting and hissing and carriage doors slamming and whistles blowing and shrill voices breaking through the tuneless drone of the crowd. Every echo, every breath of the coal-fired air, every jostle against bodies in the crowd swirling about the main concourse of this huge reeking hall, thrilled me. The wall beside the ticket wicket announced schedules and destination and fares. I could safely ignore them all. For the moment, I cared little about where I was going, and had forgotten why.

Wherever you looked you saw women and children: women lopsided with suitcases and trailed by their brood or tugging small children; older children lugging younger children; women in dark blue uniforms and bright Red Cross armbands calling out names and gesticulating directions. There were few men about, some in khaki, and an occasional policeman.

Having seen us safely to the station, father kissed our mother, kissed us and told us to 'be good childer for yir Mammy', said he would come to see us as soon as he could, and left for the shipyard. He could be killed in a blitz while we were away, I thought. But I didn't say so to him, nor to anybody else. On the station wall a poster displaying a burning ship warned us: CARELESS TALK COSTS LIVES. Fastened to the railings behind which trains waited for their human cargo, another silently interrogated us: IS YOUR JOURNEY REALLY NECESSARY? I looked for the familiar posters of beaches and mountain vistas and market towns, but they had been removed.

Mother presented her card to a uniformed woman seated at one of the long tables close to the railway platforms. I couldn't hear her conversation with my mother above the clamour around me. She wrote our names and numbers on labels, gave one to each of us and in a swanky voice instructed us to tie it to the top buttonhole of our overcoats. She directed us toward a platform alongside the stockyard that usually held cattle, pigs and sheep on their way to the docks or slaughterhouse, but now held herds of children and their mothers. We pushed and feinted our way through the crowd and were steered by another woman in uniform to an enclosure where other evacuees clustered. The place still smelt of animal pish and dung.

'Where are we goin', Mammy?'

'She didn't tell me.'

'Are we goin' t'a farm or a town?'

'I don't know. We'll see when we git there.'

After a wait of minutes or maybe an hour – in the pandemonium time had fled elsewhere – a Red Cross volunteer led us to a train where people were cramming into carriages and slamming doors behind them. We shuffled and shoved our way with other evacuees into an empty carriage.

'Where're we goin', Mammy?'

'Somewhere in Armagh.'

'Have we iver been to Armagh, Mammy?'

'No.'

'Saint Patrick's buried there,' I said.

She didn't answer me, and having exhausted my knowledge of County Armagh, I added:

'It's like a mystery excursion, Mammy.'

Except, I thought, we weren't coming back home for a while.

The train slowly clacked its way along a gauntlet of the cramped back yards of narrow streets. The dawn had not lied. Sunlight glanced off narrow windows and threw triangles of light into the dingy yards of row housing. Here and there, a line of washing like holiday bunting spanned a narrow yard. Not everybody was leaving. Now and again we passed the shell of a factory and the rubble of what had once been a street.

At the city's outskirts the train picked up speed, as if anxious to leave behind the memory of the last few weeks. We raced by the back gardens of neat semi-detached houses. From time to time a woman at her back door, or an old man on his knees between beds of sprouting cabbages or carrots, waved to us. We waved back. Then the city and civility passed out of sight. The sun rose higher above us, and I wondered when I might throw off my overcoat.

Field succeeded field without the glimpse of a horizon or stretch of sea. Cows and sheep scattered in passing fields raised their heads to stare at us thundering by, and silently we stared back, having abandoned our earlier enthusiasms on sighting them as though we had never seen such beasts before. An occasional horse frightened by the train galloped toward the farthest reaches of a field. For a while, we seemed trapped forever between embankments. In spite of the slightly open window, the carriage felt stuffy. I loosened the belt of my overcoat.

'Are we nearly there, Mammy?'

'I don't know, son.'

From time to time the train stopped, and there was much shouting and slamming of doors and shuffling of feet and thronging of platforms. At each stop, we repeated our litany:

'Do we git off here?'

'No, ye have 'til wait 'til they tell ye to git off.'

We ate our sandwiches. The train hissed, creaked, cranked, and sped on, with each click and clack along the track measuring the distance from home. Then our long wait ended.

At a station a woman rapped on the door of our carriage, shouted something in a well-bred voice to my mother, and pointed. We tumbled out of the carriage, rushed to the station lavatory, and then were ushered on board a nearby bus by a woman dressed like a man from the waist up and in a long tweed skirt from the waist down. The bus had wooden seats and we took two near the back.

'Where are we, Mammy?'

'God only knows.'

'Where's the seashore? I don't see any seashore.'

'There isn't any seashore. We're in the middle of Armagh.'

'Cin I take off my overcoat nigh?'

'No, we're nat there yit an' ye might leave it on th' bus.'

'Where we goin', Mammy?'

'I don't know. Nigh don't ask me a gain. Ye have m'head turned with yur questions.'

The bus rattled and farted, rose and fell like a roller coaster along the twisting hilly country road. My stomach rose with each hill and dropped with each dip of the road, and sloshed from left to right and right to left as the bus careened around corners. My bum slid back and forth across the slats of the seat until it felt numb. Nausea surged from my depths and hit the back of my throat. I whispered to my mother:

'I'm sick.'

'Take off yur overcoat an' loosen yur tie.'

I did, but it was too late.

'Im goin' t'boke.'

My mother shouted to the well-dressed woman, who was a volunteer recruited from among the local *polloi* to assist with delivering evacuees to their destinations:

'Could ye stap, please, stap the bus? This chile's sick.'

The bus creaked to a halt. To the astonishment of other passengers on the bus, a small body bolted down the aisle to the door, one hand jammed across his mouth, threw himself off the bus, and heaved the contents of his stomach into a ditch. With her hand my mother cupped my forehead until I had finished. Ashen and mortified, and avoiding the eyes of my fellow travellers, I shambled down the mile-long silence to my seat. The bus shuddered into life, and left the roadside mess behind.

Not long afterwards, it stopped again and a well-dressed voice shrilled, 'Morrisons!' We gathered ourselves and our gas masks and our luggage together to disembark. We had arrived.

But, then, for a moment, that seemed in some doubt.

Chapter 5

CORNAGRALLY HOUSE

THROUGH THE window of the bus I could see a tall thin-faced woman, her greying hair tied into a tight bun behind her head, her narrow body wrapped in a flowered pinafore, standing stiffly at the entrance of a lane. She wore water boots, or what could be seen of them for their tops disappeared under the hem of her black dress. The boots were streaked with mud. Nearby, a horse with enormous hooves, bigger than any I had seen on the horses that pulled carts up and down our street, idled between the shafts of a high two-wheeled cart in which a pair of milk cans leaned against a high tailboard. On the bench behind the horse's rump, the reins slack in his hand, sat a stout man wearing a cloth cap. His size and posture reminded me of my Granda Morrison, a lump of a man who filled his armchair tightly from arm to arm and sagged in it like a sack of potatoes, but who, when standing up, looked as formidable as a policeman. There the resemblance ended. The man wore a collarless shirt buttoned at the neck with a stud and dark serge trousers held up with a pair of broad braces. His shirt sleeves were rolled halfway up his forearms. Neither the man nor the woman resembled anybody on our street.

The volunteer got off the bus, said something to the woman in the pinny, who suddenly became agitated. She raised her arms and let them fall, waved her hands at nothing in particular then slapped them against her sides. We sensed something was wrong, and halted our shuffle down the aisle. My mother, thinking perhaps that she was somehow to blame, said something about a mix-up. The volunteer shook her head, and her well-dressed chest heaved:

'Mrs Morrison, the evacuation has been a bloody mix-up since it started.'

She signalled to us, we filed off the bus, and were introduced to Jinny Hale.

A minute later the bus, as if anxious to escape a barney, disappeared around one of the thousands of bends in the roads that twist the Irish countryside – and tender stomachs – into the coils of a Celtic tapestry. I took a deep sniff, but there wasn't a whiff of sea wrack in the air.

Jinny Hale looked upset. The man on the cart seemed amused. We were perplexed. Our mother again apologised for the mistake she hadn't made, but Jinny dismissed it. 'Ooch', she said and folded her arms tightly against her chest as if she had no further need of them. She released one hand to gesticulate in our direction:

'Th' childer must be starvin'.'

She spoke sharply, like a headmistress with an odd accent, and nodded towards the man on the cart,

'That's Mr Hale. Victor, take thim t'th' hause.'

I looked up at Victor. His half-open mouth held the trace of a smile, as if he was unsure how to welcome us, and I knew instinctively that the Hales had no children. In an accent as odd as his wife's he broke his silence:

'D'ye want t'ride t'th'hause in th'ceart?'

The question was not a command in disguise; his gruff voice, rising in a lilt, was as casual as if we were his grandchildren. We didn't answer and looked towards our mother.

'Go on youse,' she nodded.

With help from Victor we clambered up the foot rest and tumbled awkwardly into the cart, our gas masks thumping against the cart's sides. His hand was rough. His boots, just inches from my face as I climbed, were clabbered worse than the woman's. Cow clap, or just muck, it was hard to tell. My shoes though a bit scuffy, still had their shine. I remembered what my father said about having clean shoes, and looked again at Victor's water boots. And wondered about my father's judgement.

Holding tightly to the side of the cart, we rode down the lane toward the house. Our mother, with Elsie in her push chair, and Jinny alongside her, followed on foot.

The afternoon sun now had inclined toward the west. A tall hawthorn hedge cast a thick narrow shadow down the lane, filling one of the ruts along which the cart bumped and swayed. We rode in silence, keeping our tongues to ourselves. Victor spoke:

'He's Dan,' he said, nodding toward the horse.

I didn't know how to say hello to a horse, so I just repeated the name as if I was being taught a new word. Norman said:

'He's got a pile of hair over his hooves.'

'Them's his fetlocks,' Victor explained.

We settled back into silence as if we had done enough talking for the day. The cart swayed and creaked.

It was like entering a fog, except it wasn't a fog. At first faint, so that I thought it must be coming from Victor's boots, then, a few yards later thick, the sweetsharp smell of animal manure closed around us. We were too polite to hold our noses, which was just as well, for we had to get used to it; unlike a fog it wasn't going away overnight. Or any other night.

The lane opened out into a farmyard as wide and deep as a small playground. Or so it seemed to me. A two storey stone grey farmhouse sat to one side of the yard, close by an orchard. It looked ancient and huge. Victor said, with a nod as though we were sight-seeing:

'That's Cornagrally House.'

None of us spoke. If our tongues had been resting during our brief ride in the cart, they were now paralysed, unable to repeat the name we had heard. We were going to live in a big house with a name which Victor seemed to half-swallow as he pronounced it. We were going to live in it until the war ended. And nobody knew when that would be. A long, long time, maybe.

In a big scullery with a stone floor – a 'proper kitchen,' our mother whispered as we gaped at its spaciousness – Jinny set about buttering slices of bread and pouring out cups of milk.

'Fresh from th' cow this marnin',' she said about the milk.

'Churned this marnin',' she added about the butter.

The slightly warm sweet milk smelled of comfort and had the touch of velvet on the tongue. The pale butter tasted salty, different from the blend our mother made from what little butter we got for our ration coupons and the more plentiful margarine. 'Makes the butter go further,' she would say, but, in truth, it only stretched the bland yellow margarine further. Jinny's butter tasted *buttery*.

While Jinny watched, we ate and drank shyly, not daring to ask for more bread when the plate emptied nor more milk when we drained our cups. We sat primly, our elbows off the table. Our mother, who didn't want people to think we were raised in a field, must have been pleased with us. What Jinny thought of the four children ranging in age from two and a half to eight years of age seated at her table, only God knows, and maybe Victor.

After we had eaten, we waited in silence to be told by our mother what do. But it was Jinny who spoke. She told us that certain parts of the house were out of bounds: the main staircase which rose grandly on carpeted treads from the hallway at the front door, and the front parlour, which she said, she kept under lock and key. We were to use always the back stairs which, uncarpeted, shot upwards from the kitchen to the landing on the upper floor where the bedrooms were. As she spoke, the glamour I had felt at the prospect of living in this big house began to leave me. Life with Jinny was not going to be fun.

Our mother took us up the back stairs to show us where we would be, as Jinny put it, 'slepping'. The bedroom was more than twice the size of ours at home, but it smelled musty, and its wallpaper looked as ancient as the wardrobe with the mirror frayed at the edges where the silver backing had peeled. A white ceramic basin and an ewer sat on a small dark table by the sash window. Over a large bed, and held aloft by four tall bedposts, a white faded fringed canopy sagged in a slight belly.

'This our bed?'

'Yis, for th' four of youse,' Mammy said. 'Hope't has no fleas in't.'

At that, we threw ourselves laughing on to the bed. Its springs creaked, but the mattress was softer than the lumpy tick at home. We leaped on it to punch the canopy above, and the springs complained. We had come to the right place even if we were at the wrong place, and even if Jinny might be troublesome. At least, we would sleep like swanks.

Our mother laid down the law more firmly than Jinny:

'We're goin' t' be here for a while, so youse are to behave yourselves. The Hales will be wantin' ye to help thim now and agane. YOU come when you're called for yur breakfast – no lyin' in bed, mister Will – an' for yur tea. An' wash yur hands before ye eat. An' always scrape th' muck off yer shoes before ye come inta th' house. As Jinny said, th' parlour downstairs is for special visitors, like th' minister, an' YOU don't go inta it. YOU don't use th' front stairs. Ye already know where th' lavetry is. If ye have to do a flood during th' night, use th' po.'

At the mention of the po we looked under the bed. It sat smugly in its white porcelain purity, capacious enough to hold a gallon of flood and whatever else might go into it, and with a handle huge enough to put your arm through. We hefted it in turn.

'Heavy.'

'Full of flood you'll need yer two hans t'carry it, for fear of splashing it down th' stairs.'

The po was returned to its complacency under the bed.

'One last thing. We're nat supposed to be here, for th' Hales wanted only one evacuee, but they're lettin' us stay. I don't want any of you disgracin' me, for God only knows where we might end up. So, mind yurselves.'

'Mammy, where are we?'

'Loughgilly.'

'Are we near th' seaside?'

'Will ye stop askin' about th' seaside: it's miles away.'

'How long will we be staying here?'

'God only knows. 'Til the war ends.'

And since He wasn't telling when that might be, I let the matter lie there. I had something more serious on my mind.

'Are we goin' t'haf t'go t'school?'

'Yis. An' git off yur good clothes. Hing yur suits in the wardrobe. Y'ill nat be needin' thim. Put on yer jerseys an' yur old trousers.'

I looked out of the bedroom window, which overlooked the farmyard, and saw in the middle of the yard, a pump with a long handle in the shape of a scimitar. It looked like a stunted apple tree, and cast a short shadow on the ground. I turned away from the window, and began unpacking my wee attaché case.

That we had been delivered to the wrong farm no longer mattered. Nor did it any longer matter that I didn't know where we were, nor how far we had come, nor where the sea was. It had been a long journey from the maimed city, and it was enough for me that we had arrived.

Chapter 6

A SUMMER'S SUN

IT WAS a time in my life when it never rained – a miracle in Northern Ireland, or a quirk of memory. Every morning the sun arose impatiently and every evening went reluctantly to bed. On some days white clouds drifted across the blue, and on others, wisps of white hair, and not so much as a tear fell. Or so it seemed. Around the farmyard, cowclapped and mud-dappled green fields spread themselves as far as the hawthorn hedges allowed. In the distance, ripening corn gently rose and fell back into the sky; and where the lane met the farmhouse, apple and pear and plum trees stood unfenced, unguarded, innocent. In a pig sty in the farmyard, and far from home, I stood with my little brother and my friend Herbie and his older brother, up to our ankles in alien clabber, and loving every minute of the pungent slopswishing days.

That in the confusion of the evacuation from the bombed city we had been dropped off the wrong place, and that no one had tried to correct the error, proved to be our good fortune. But whether Jinny would agree with me, is another matter entirely.

On the day after our arrival on the farm, Norman, Mavis and I hand-in-hand roamed the yard and fields. We learned the difference between a byre and a barn, we saw how the pigs were fed and cows milked, and we wandered among the apple and pear and plum trees in an orchard bigger than any on the avenue near our street in Belfast. Those orchards, glimpsed through high hedges as we passed along the avenue, tempted us to rob them, at our peril. Here, on the farm, we looked up into the thick foliage loaded with apples and pears the size of baby fists, and surmised only when we might pick them.

Near the byre we met Jimmy. He and Victor were tossing pitchforks of horse dung into a sloppy foul pile of manure. Jimmy was smaller than Victor, and his clabbered gum boots rose to his knees. His cloth cap, the size of a bin lid, stuck out from his head like the eaves of a roof. Victor nodded towards him.

'That's Jimmy,' and to Jimmy he said, 'Th' wee childer fram Belfast I wis tellin' ye aboot.'

Jimmy nodded, and smiled as if he was about to laugh. The peak of his cap overshadowed his eyes. Since he didn't speak, we said nothing and shyly moved on to see the pigs. Later that day I learned that Jimmy, the Hale's farm hand, was a Roman Catholic. Maybe that was why he didn't speak to us, I thought. Or was it because he was a farm hand? I was confused, for Jimmy intrigued me.

In the evenings of that first week, we loitered by the byre while Victor and Jimmy, yipping, clacking their tongues, and flicking willow switches, cajoled a small herd of cows out of a field and into the farmyard. The beasts moved slowly, as if they weren't to be hurried, their huge wicked horned heads nodding benignly, their claptatted tails curling in the air, and swollen udders swinging in rhythm with their ponderous gait which, though slow, seemed to have such purpose that I believed the cows, if left alone, would find their own way into the byre.

Early one morning we went to the byre to see the milking. The sharp smell of cow's urine made the eyes water, but did not deter us, for we were becoming used to the smells of the farmyard. We picked our way delicately, like birds in a garden after a rainfall, across the straw matted dirt floor toward the row of massive cowclapped haunches where, in a stall, Jimmy sat on a stool with the side of his head pressed against a cow's flanks. His duncher was askew, so that I could now see his large dark eyes. The cow lowed in complaint or content, its tail scrolling in the air to some music only it could hear. When we sensed we were in no danger, we edged closer to Jimmy until we looking over his shoulder. His hands rhythmically tugged on a pair of teats, from which thin streams of milk, like jets from a water pistol, splashed into a bucket wedged between his knees. The other teats hung idly, like discoloured sausages in a butcher's window. A faint sweet steam arose from the froth.

All of a sudden, Jimmy flicked his wrist and a jet of milk shot in our direction. Yelping, we leapt back. Jimmy looked up.

'Lik t'try it?' he asked. His accent was more country than Victor's, softer. I nodded:

'Yis.'

Dodging the flicks of the shit-caked tail, I seated myself on the stool, and tentatively closed my hand around the teat. Its warmth and suppleness startled me, and I released my grip. Then I grabbed it and jerked, as I would a chain to flush a toilet. The cow bellowed, its rump heaved, its tail cracked like a whip, and a hoof lifted off the floor. Jimmy quickly intervened, and showed me how to draw the milk from the teat, and I tried, but not a drop issued.

'Maybe the cow has to know you,' I said.

Jimmy said nothing, just nodded his head, but he seemed amused by my failure, and I resolved never to try again.

We moved to the stall where Victor was sitting.

'Lik yer malk straight fram th' cow?' he asked.

The vowel in 'cow' rose and fell as if split in two. We nodded.

'Ope yir mouths,' he said.

We stepped forward, one after the other, and bent agape toward the cow's udder. The milk hit the roof of my mouth like a warm blunt knitting needle, and spilled down my throat and splashed my jersey. I spluttered, wiped my wet mouth on the sleeve of my jersey. We laughed, and Victor beamed. At the door of the byre I turned. Jimmy's head was still pressed against a cow, but he was watching us, and smiling.

Throughout the first week of our new life on the farm we stayed out of mischief, except for chasing the chickens, especially the black ones that strutted about the farmyard and around the house. When Jinny caught us she scolded us sharply:

'Don't chase th'hens. Yi'll put thim aff alayin'.'

Then, as if regretting her peevishness, she said:

'Here, come ta th'hen-hause. I'll show ye whur they lay th'eggs, an' ye cin gather thim for me each marnin'.'

The hen-house, constructed of boards from which a dirty white paint was flaking, sat at the end of a chicken run in a field behind the farmhouse. On our entrance, hens on the wide straw-lined shelves around the walls broke into a protest of raucous clucking and flapping of wings that sent swirls of dust and shards of straw into the acrid air. I felt my chest tightening. Their beady eyes swiveled in their bobbing heads like miniature pinwheels, and in their nippous cackling beaks you could see their tongues fluttering like tiny pink flames blown in a breeze.

One fact of farm life suddenly became clear; it was one thing to chase a creature in the farmyard, where you had room to run away if it chose to face you; being cooped up with them in a hen-house or byre or sty was another matter entirely. We stayed close to Jinny. She pointed out a fellow in black velvet and a large scarlet comb and magnificent tail, standing on the edge of a shelf, saying nothing, keeping his wings to himself, but never taking his eyes off us. I took note of his beak and claws, and edged closer behind Jinny as she nudged hens out of their nests and lifted their eggs from the dimpled straw.

'Th' hens won't peck ye if ye don't frighten thim. Just push thim gently. There, like that. An' luk around outside in the long grass. Some hens lik t'lay eggs there.'

The farm was littered with feathers, much to my delight. In the city, they were hard to find. After you had seen Geronimo and the Apaches at the picture house, you scoured gardens and gutters for any feather, the dull black of a crow or the dirty white of a pigeon. Sparrow feathers were plentiful, but useless, being too small. At the seaside you found grey seagull feathers trampled into the sand. Making a full war bonnet was out of the question; so, you settled for two or three feathers which you cherished until they became so bedraggled your mother made you throw them in the bin.

Here, on the farm, every day there were enough feathers of every hue for a chief's bonnet: auburn, black, white, and feathers tinted with red or purple. A brown hen is an unremarkable brown bird, until you notice the bronze and auburn of its fantail. I gathered a fistful and went into the house to find a ribbon, to tie them into a war bonnet. My mother was in the kitchen.

'What're ye doin' with them feathers?'

'Making a war bonnet, Mammy. Like Geronimo's.'

'Wash them before ye bring them in here.'

'But they're clean, Mammy. They're hens' feathers.'

'Hens carry nits an' fleas an' you'll be bringin' thim in. Wash thim at th' pump.'

I took the feathers out to the pump in the yard and ran them under the water. I couldn't see any nits or fleas, and the feathers now looked pitiful, like hair combs with broken teeth, and I was annoyed with my mother. I laid them on the bedroom window sill to dry, in the hope that they would recover their lustrous glory, and gazed out toward a distant hill. I let my mind drift to a darkened cinema, to Geronimo, in full war bonnet and gripping a lance bedecked with feathers, sitting on a horse more magnificent than Dan, even with his fetlocks. And I remembered my chums, with whom I raced the streets and whooped in the back field behind our houses. Where had they been sent? I wondered. When would I see them again? I thought of the school in Loughgilly. Maybe, I'll make friends there, have country chums.

I had hoped that, since we had been evacuated so late in the school year, we wouldn't be expected to attend school, but my mother and whoever else had control of my life had decided otherwise. Mullaghmore Public Elementary School, in which Norman and I were enrolled shortly after our arrival in Loughgilly, was a grey stone building with two classrooms and two teachers: Miss Gray, who taught the lower Standards, and Mr Henning, the headmaster, who taught the higher Standards. We would be in the Lower Standards. The older and bigger pupils were in the Higher Standards.

On our first morning at school, Miss Gray and Mr Henning introduced us to the assembled pupils as evacuees from the Blitz and were now far from home. He welcomed us, and told the assembled pupils to make us feel welcome in Mullaghmore. The pupils must have been deaf. In the playground at lunch time, a few hefty lumps in the Upper Standards passed the word to a couple of boys in the Lower Standard, who passed it on to us: 'Them big boys is goin'a git ye.' I felt what a seaman must have felt in Lord Nelson's Navy, on being sentenced to a flogging without being told when it would happen.

At Everton School I more or less ignored threats of being 'git' by someone for they often came to nothing, and when they did come to something I always could always count on my chums jumping into the fight. At Mullaghmore, Norman and I were on our own. I lay awake that night longer than usual, and in the morning I awoke in a state of terror.

It was a long walk from the farm to the school. We crossed a couple of fields, and then took the road that rose to the brow of the hill where the school stood. Here and there tall hawthorn hedges blocked our view of turns in the road ahead, and so we stayed alert to any signs of an ambush, and hoped with each step that these Loughgilly louts were too lazy to ambush us before school.

Each day for two weeks, I waited for the violent shove in the playground, a fist in the eye or square on the nose, or a stone on the back of the head. Then, one day, my terror came to an end.

Our next-door neighbours in Belfast, the Hynes family, had the misfortune, like some evacuees, of being placed in a dreadful home in the town of Newry. When my mother learned of their misery, she talked Jinny into taking them. Mrs Hynes had three children: Herbie, my best friend, a month younger than me but hefty and tough, Bobby, twelve-years-old and big, and Vi, her ten-year-old daughter. We now had our own gang.

The phoney war at school came to an end one afternoon after school. On the road back to the farm, we heard shouts behind us, and turned. Several boys began pitching stones toward us, expecting us to run from them. But we denied them that moral victory. Picking up whatever stones we could find, we hurled them with such ferocity that our attackers turned tail and ran, one or two yelping as a bouncing stone caught a leg. They had chosen the wrong kind of battle and the wrong battlefield. After all, clodding stones was a city boy's most popular sport, and by the same token, dodging falling stones was a honed skill. There were few skirmishes after that, and none did damage.

On the school playground too, we held our ground, exchanging insults, threats, and sometimes tangling in a wrestle. Mr Henning had the knack of appearing at a critical moment, so that no nose was bloodied nor eye bruised. But the rancour between us and the Loughgilly boys remained; we made no friends at school, and as far as I was concerned, that no longer mattered.

Miss Gray was tall, or so it seemed, and she looked to be the age of our mother. She flowed about the room in a summer dress that occasionally brushed my desk as she passed. She was kindly, lenient, and would leave the class unattended from time to time, trusting us to keep our heads bent over our sums or copybooks or readers, and to stay out of mischief, until she returned. Used as we were to the strict teachers and regimented classroom behaviour at our schools in Belfast, we couldn't resist the temptation to take advantage, not of Miss Gray, for we were diligent pupils, but of opportunities afforded by the relaxed atmosphere of the school.

Within a short time, we acquired a hoard of pilfered nibs, erasers and chalk. We didn't steal them to sell, but because they were lying neatly in their boxes, begging to be taken. Emboldened by success, I plundered Miss Gray's desk drawer, found a ball of twine I thought would be useful, and slipped it into my pocket.

Sometimes, Miss Gray mused that there should be more chalk in her box, and was puzzled, she said, at how few nibs and erasers were left in the cupboard. She seemed to have misplaced her ball of string, she said, but couldn't for the life of her think of where. I gazed at her, blushed, and hoped that she wouldn't notice me.

But like most thieves, we overreached. One afternoon, as Miss Gray was preparing the class for art, she discovered she was short of paint brushes and pots of poster paint. She asked if anyone had taken them home. No hand went up. It was odd, she said. At that, I realised it would be wise to end our pilfering, for Miss Gray was about to become a detective.

Herbie, Norman and I dallied in front of her desk until the classroom emptied. We admitted to taking home the paint and brushes, offered as an excuse our belief that we could borrow them to use at home, and apologised. Miss Gray was gracious, didn't test our belief for its untruth, said something about evacuees being strange to the ways of a country school, and cautioned us not to repeat the offence. She said nothing about the missing nibs, erasers, and chalk, nor did we. We had done enough confessing for one day, and we didn't want her to think we were budding Borstal boys.

The following morning, we returned the paints and brushes, and during one of Miss Gray's frequent absences from the classroom, we surreptitiously put back nibs, unused erasers and what remained of the chalk. As for the ball of string, I kept it, because Miss Gray seemed convinced that she had misplaced it and had never mentioned it again, and besides, I had use for it.

Whatever qualms I had about my failure to make a complete confession and full restitution of ill-gotten goods soon dissipated. For within days, school was out; our summer holiday had begun. And it would be a long holiday, we learned to our joy, for there was a harvest to be gathered and every boy and girl was needed to help bring it in. I never saw Miss Gray nor Mr Henning again, nor the boys who once had terrorised me.

Unlike weekdays, Sundays on the farm were quiet, and unlike our Sundays in Belfast, churchless. Neither of our mothers were churchgoers, yet we were forbidden boisterous play, so as not to offend Jinny who was a strict Reformed Presbyterian, of the old Scottish variety. We lay in our bedroom or sat in the kitchen reading, the parlour being out of bounds, or wandered aimlessly about the Sabbath farm until the sun stretched its languorous legs into the evening and the long long hours sank into night. I came to feel that even church would be a change from the monotony of Sabbath, for churchgoing meant riding in the cart since the nearest church, which Jinny and Victor attended, was quite a distance away.

One balmy Sunday morning our mother told us that after the dutiful morning chores around the farm were done – since hens and cows and pigs were not Presbyterians – we could go to church with Victor and Jinny. Late in the morning, for God was not worshipped nor importuned before eleven o'clock, we set off in a cart swept clean for the occasion, and drawn by Dan, he of the magnificent, white, dependable fetlocks: my mother, Victor, Jinny, and the gang, all in our Sunday best and smelling faintly of camphor.

In the small Reformed Church, reformed in the sense of going back to a

Presbyterian past before such diabolical inventions as the church organ and the dubious theology of hymns corrupted true worship, we sang a capella the psalms of David from a Psalter which contained metrical psalms in tonic solfa for the tenors and sopranos, altos and basses sprinkled among the congregation. The Psalter's pagination was such that you could match any tune to any psalm. Sometimes, the little choir and congregation drew out every syllable of a line as if to lose even one would send the rest scattering like pearls from a broken necklace; at other times, the cantor whose voice led the rest like the bass of a pipe organ, set a steady pace and the psalm raced along with a spirited air.

Then came the sermon, the Word, the climax of the service as in our city church. We settled in the pew, for it would be long, God having so much to say to us. Sunlight pressed through the diamonds of stained and frosted glass in a window close by to where we sat. The late morning warmth, the odour of varnish from the auburn pew in front of me, the drone of the frock-coat in the distant pulpit, blended in a heady soporific from which I drowsily sipped, so that my next moment of awareness was a nudge from my mother to stand for the singing of the psalm before the Benediction, which sent us home.

The journey home in the early afternoon was slow, as if somehow the service had sapped our energy. Even Dan, who for the last hour and a half had been tethered to a tree and left alone with his own thoughts, seemed tired. At each sharp rise in the road we climbed down from the cart to ease his lot, and we trailed alongside it, plucking leaves from time to time from the hawthorn hedgerows and chewing them and marvelling to one another that they should taste so fragrant. It had been a long time since breakfast.

With our fathers absent, Mr Hynes in the army and my father at home in Belfast because he still worked in the shipyard, our mothers had full authority over us, much as they had back home, anyway, and so little had really changed in matters of law and order, and punishment, as far as we were concerned. The authority over us should have been Victor, since he owned the farm, but his name, which suggests authority as well as strength, belied his easygoing nature. Victor had little to say to us on the day we arrived, and in the weeks that followed added little more, so that if you put down in writing all he said, you might have half a page, in large print. And that might include any instructions he gave us about our chores.

We feared our mothers' wrath, but it was Jinny's anger and displeasure that deterred us when we were tempted to lawlessness. For a short while, at least.

Chapter 7

'THEM BOYS!'

JINNY HAD offered to take temporarily into her life one evacuee. Then she took four. Within a couple of weeks, she had seven children roaming the farm and sleeping in her house. Into the bargain, she had two married women under her roof, and although neither one was a daughter-in-law, she had to cope with them, for neither my mother nor Mrs Hynes were the kind of women who would hold their tongues if they were cross, or if their offspring were not being properly treated.

My mother thought that Jinny didn't give us enough bread, but we were never hungry; eggs came in endless supply, milk in gallons, and if bread was rationed among us at least we had butter on it rather than tasteless 'marge'. Jinny had a large garden, which furnished us with a variety of vegetables. We had no sweets or chocolate, but if we felt hunger, we would slip into the garden for peas and beans fresh from the pod, and a sweet-smelling carrot. Besides, apples and pears were ripening with each passing day, and even a sour apple was a thousand times more delectable than cabbage. And if Jinny skimped on bread, she made up for it with juicy apple pies as thick as bricks.

As I romped around the farm I gave only fleeting thought to Jinny's generosity in taking so many evacuees. Sometimes, when we dallied with mischief, our mother would remind us that Jinny had gone far beyond what was expected of her, and if we caused too much trouble we would be sent home. I wasn't anxious to be sent home; life on the farm was good, even if Jinny's presence, seen and unseen, moved among us.

To us, she was an old woman (in fact, she wasn't) who didn't understand us (in fact, she may have, but we thought we had evidence that she did not). She wore every day, it seemed, the same pinafore we saw on the day of our arrival, over the same black dress, and a pair of water boots that perpetually hid her legs, so that she might have walked on stilts, for all we knew. And her voice was tuned to high doh. She wasn't exactly the witch in the woods, but, like the God we heard about in Sunday school back in the city, she was the ONE WE HAD TO WATCH OUT FOR. And with that perversity which is common to children, because we feared her, we tormented her. Not intentionally, but inevitably, which comes to the same thing, I suppose.

Our fall from grace begins on an idyllic morning, when, at Jinny's bidding, three boys and two girls, with a wicker basket, set about collecting newly laid eggs in and around the hen-house. It isn't a chore; it's more like a treasure hunt, because some hens prefer to lay eggs outside the hen-house. Besides, you have a chance to terrorise them, watch them flap and squawk in fright. But you keep your distance from the roosters.

We gather the eggs laid in the roost, and then set about finding those laid by contrary hens in the long grass around the hen run. The meadow bathes in early sunlight, a few white clouds float in the blue above. God is in his heaven, and if somewhere armies clash, on this lovely morning we have forgotten them. We fan out among the long grass, the hens cluck and run in erratic circles around us.

Herbie shouts, 'Here's one' and turning toward me yells 'Catch!' I catch it gently, swinging my hands to the motion of the pitch as one does with a cricket ball. Another is found, lobbed unexpectedly, and this time caught like a tennis ball, tightly. Yolk and whites drip from fingers. Norman catches one too close to his chest. 'Hand grenade!' I shout, and an egg aimed high smashes against the hen house wall. Mavis and Vi try to protect the eggs in the basket. Hens race to and fro like a crowd in panic, unable to make sense of what they see. We turn on the black ones, shout 'Natzes!' and scare the living daylights out of them.

By the time we recover our reason the walls of the hen house run yellow as if a mad artist has painted murals of sunbursts. Bits of eggshells have stuck to the boards where egg white is gelling.

Appalled by the sight, Herbie, Norman and I leave Mavis and Vi to return the basket containing the remaining eggs to Jinny in the kitchen, and we take refuge among the apple trees in the orchard. The hens have ceased squawking, a pastoral quiet falls on the field. Midges congregate in the air, and the world is as it should be, except for the eggshells that litter the ground like tiny crushed skulls.

Noticing that there are fewer eggs in the basket than is usual, and thinking that we have shirked our work, Jinny tramps to the hen house. Suddenly, the morning disintegrates. Jinny's voice shrieks over the roof tops, startling small birds that wheel from under the eaves into the twittering air.

'Missus Marrisen! Missus Hynes! Missus Marrisen! Missus Hynes!'

Her arms flapping in full flight, Jinny bounds in her water boots between the hen house and our mothers, all the while keeping up a loud lament.

'Och, them boys, them bad bad boys. They've broke me eggs, they've broke me eggs. All over th' hen hause, all over th' hen hause.'

Our mothers try to calm her with apologies for our behaviour, and then call for us in shrill wrath-laden voices, and we slouch from the orchard, trembling, and trying to look repentant. Jinny, finally subdued, without another word tramps back to the hen-house.

We pick up the broken egg shells and wash the hen-house walls as best we can, and spend the rest of the day confined to our bedroom. The next morning faint yellow streaks are still visible on the dirty white walls of the hen house, and will remain, I suppose, until either grime or fresh paint or decay finally erases them.

For a few days afterwards, Jinny doesn't say a word to us. Nor we to her. 'Sorry' seems insufficient and, we know, insincere.

Shooting flaming arrows in the barn is my idea, and Herbie and Norman are keen on it. It would be like the attack on the hen house, but less messy. That the barn might catch fire never crosses my mind, because, except for some hay in the loft, it is empty. Besides, it is built of stone.

We often play there; climb the ladder into the loft and dive into the hay, shoot marbles on the dirt floor, leapfrog the length of the barn, and, on days when the fields are too wet for us to fight alongside Geronimo, we send arrows into straw targets set up at one end of it, for we have bows cut from saplings and strung with the cord I had filched from Miss Gray's desk, and arrows cut from slender shoots of willow, their tips weighted with twists of chicken wire.

Loughgilly is perfect Indian country; the sky boundless and the fields expansive, in our eyes, at least. We can shoot arrows without anxiety until our arms flop and our fingers blister from the twang of the bowstring. There are no houses nearby, whose roofs might trap the arrows in eaves troughs, nor windows through which an errant arrow might pass to thud on the picture of King George VI and his Queen hanging on a kitchen wall, or worse, into King Billy on his white horse.

The afternoon of the catastrophe is wet, dull, and the farmyard is muddy, and so Herbie, Bobby, Norman and I gather in the barn with our bows and arrows. We make a small stook of straw at one end of the barn, tie stalks of straw to our arrow tips, and light them with matches pilfered from the house. From a position near the barn door each of us shoots a burning arrow into the stook. Streamers of smoke begin to rise from it, then flames. We whoop and jig, and fail to notice that smoke is drifting out of the barn, until a scream, pitched at an unmistakable high doh, roots us for an instant to where we dance.

'Th' barn's on fire! Th' barn's on fire!'

Through the open door we see Jinny racing toward the barn as fast as her water boots will allow. We scatter the burning stook, and stamp the stalks until the flames go out. My mother arrives with a bucket of water. Disgusted with Jinny's alarums, we assure my mother 'It's only some straw, an' it's out,' but she throws the water on the ashes anyway. Outside the barn Jinny, a note short of hysterics, shuffles back and forth in her water boots as if she is trying to cut a rut in the ground.

'Them childer! Och them childer, agin, Missus Marrisen. They've m'heart broke. Bad boys, such bad boys. They'll have to go back t' Belfast.'

Victor and Jimmy appear. Jinny gestures toward us as if chasing off flies.

'They near burned down th' barn, Victor. Such bad boys.'

Victor comes into the barn, his large blue eyes wide open as if he has seen a ghost or is in a state of wonder. He looks around, looks at us, says nothing, and leaves. Jimmy smiles slightly, and trails after him. My mother takes control.

'Back t'th'house, youse. Gimme them bows an' arras.'

'Cin we have our bows back tamarra?'

'No more bows an' arras for youse boys. Ye scared the livin' lights outa Jinny.'

Jinny does not press her case, and we are not sent back to Belfast. It is a long while before another arrow sails into the sky over Loughgilly, or a small band of small warriors trail after the ghost of Geronimo.

It is at the end of a market day in August that we test Jinny's forbearance to the limits, and risk most gravely our exile from Eden. On market days we stayed at the farm, much to our disappointment. I wondered what was so mysterious about those days, because my mother could not give me a better reason for not going than that we would be in Victor and Jimmy's way, and that anyway Jinny needed to be free from us for a while. She promised that we would have our own excursion by bus to Markethill, the nearest town to the farm, and was as good as her word.

The road to Markethill is the same road along which we had travelled to Hale's farm so long ago, it seems, but in fact, barely three months have passed. And the bus is the same bone shaker with washboard seats. We browse the town, buy a few sweets, the first we have had in a long time, with our sweetie coupons. In a chemist shop, where our mother buys some castor oil and cough medicine, we beg for cinnamon sticks, and she buys four, two of which are for Bobby and Herbie. Before catching the bus back to Loughgilly, we have chips with bread and butter and a pot of tea, in a little café.

At the end of the tea, our mother wraps up the left over slices of bread in a piece of newspaper and slips them surreptitiously into her handbag. 'A bit t'eat on th' bus' she says, and we giggle and muse aloud what she will say to the woman at the till. But she says nothing, and we feel, as we file out of the restaurant, that we have been conspirators in our mother's little 'crime'.

On the back seat of the bus to Loughgilly, we 'ooh' and 'aah' in unison with every fall and rise of the road and laugh at our foolishness, and don't care if the other passengers think we are rowdies. I will my stomach to keep its chips and tea in check, and it does.

The evening is warm, the sun low in the sky. Midges, like motes caught in shafts of sunlight, dance underneath the trees in the orchard where, with Bobbie and Herbie, Norman and I loiter, cinnamon sticks wriggling in our mouths as we nibble on the hard aromatic bark. We imagine ourselves to be toughs puffing on Woodbines. Victor and Jinny have not yet returned from the market.

'We should be smokin' these sticks, like we do in th' back field,' Herbie says.

The back field behind our houses in Belfast is our turf. I gaze at the farmhouse, and Herbie reads my thoughts.

'She keeps it locked. We'd nat get in. Anyway she'd have hysterics if we did,' he says.

But the idea is enough to draw us toward the house, and we dander around it until we are outside the parlour window. There is no one about the farmyard. The bottom of the lower sash is within our reach: Herbie casually tries to raise the sash and to our surprise, it slides upwards. Within a minute, all of us are over the window sill.

The parlour smells of camphor. In the gloom, for we keep the curtains drawn, and certain our entry has not been seen, we light up. The cinnamon doesn't burn readily, and it is a while before I'm able to get a good draw of smoke, which I hold in my mouth and then release, and breathe up my nose. We sprawl on the armchairs and horse hair sofa, and I see myself as James Cagney, for he is small and scrawny like me. Whatever the roguish image each of us has of himself, at its heart lies a sweet sense of self-congratulation with this one symbolic defiance of Jinny.

Caught up in euphoria of our daring and our hell-bent efforts to get a decent draw from our fegs, we fail to take into account that the odour of cinnamon might drift beyond the door of the parlour. Nor do we pay attention to the creaking of a passing cart.

Unexpectedly, the parlour door opens. Jinny stands framed in the doorway against the dull light of the hallway. We jump to our feet. Jinny lifts up her voice, and pierces the mellow spicy air like a dagger.

'Missus Marisen! Missus Hynes!'
Our mothers' faces appear over Jinny's shoulder.

'Them Boys!'

'Them boys. I wis goin by th' parlour dure an I cud smell something coming from in there, an there they were, lying about in my chairs smokin' as you please. An' them knowing they're not allowed inta th' parlour. How'd they git in?'

My mother pushes past Jinny into the parlour:

'Youse know you shouldn't be in there?'

Silence.

'How'd youse get in?'

'Th' windy was open.'

'Gimme them sticks. Youse could've burnt th' house down.'

'We were careful.'

'Th' one thing youse was told nat t'do, youse did. Youse disgraced me. Upstairs youse.'

We file into the hallway, not looking at Jinny. She is muttering something. My mother snaps:

'Nat up them front stairs, up th' back!'

We leave our mothers to sort out and soothe Jinny's mutterings, and go to our bedroom to await our punishment. It is swift and severe. I don't know what has happened to Herbie and Bobby, but my mother has a cane, and she wallops the backs of my legs and thighs while I yelp and dance to the rhythm of her swings. Norman gets off lightly, with a cuff on the ear, for, she says, he is little and is led astray by me and Herbie. And saying that, she gives me another whack, and orders us to stay in the room until morning. No tea for us.

Later, after our sniffles subside, Norman and I lie on the bed biting into apples we had stuffed in our pockets while in the orchard, and leaning out of the bed we toss the butts into the mirthful darkness, and listen for their quiet fall into the canopy above us.

Chapter 8

HARVEST HOME

WITH THE approach of harvest, a calm settled on our relations with Jinny. We learned to stook the corn that fell in swathes before the reaping machine drawn by Dan and the scythes swung by men, sleeves rolled up to their shoulders, arms tanned by the sun, which seemed to preside over those days. Their scythes sighed in rhythm across the field where the reaping machine left off, golden stands falling before them as a strong wet wind lays flat the tall grasses in its path. It was a glorious sight, even to my young eyes.

We carried lunches and tea cans to the workers in the fields, neighbours of the Hales, and sat beside them on the prickly stubble, eating our sandwiches. It was as if we were at the seaside and the golden fields around us were the sea, and the sweet smell of mown corn the brine of spin drift and the chlorine of kelp.

On one bright afternoon we heard a shout from Victor on the reaper, and we left our stooking to see what he was pointing at. Jinny called out, her voice anxious: 'Don't let the childer see it!' But she called too late. Beneath a swath of barley lay a brown and white bundle of bloody fur, a luckless rabbit, paralysed by terror perhaps, and then caught by the blades of the reaper. The sun glinted on the small scarlet pools oozing over the fallen stalks. What I saw, though I didn't know it then, foreshadowed a day that came too soon to the farmyard.

Of all the creatures on the farm, the pigs enthralled us the most. Not even the antics of the goat, which we pestered to charge us – which it never did for it was a patient old billy – gave us more pleasure than the rambunctious pigs slopswilling their days away until their doom. Their hedonistic heaven had a sinister secret, and I half-believed they knew it, for they took every chance to escape the sty into the open fields.

Cleaning the pigsty was a job we asked for, begged for, and when given, never shirked. Victor had no experience of mixing large pigs with small boys; and so, at first he was reluctant to let us into the sty, for the pigs, eight or ten of them, were hefty brutes. Jinny was afraid the pigs might bite us, or maybe, that we would bite or cripple the pigs. We implored Victor with assurances that we would be careful, and neither tease the pigs nor let them out.

At feed-time, they were penned in their shed while Victor and Jimmy filled the trough with buckets of sour-smelling warm slop. At the word from Victor, one of us, as doorkeeper, would open the shed door and skip aside smartly, because the pigs stampeded toward the trough, the bigger ones shunting aside the smaller. Plunging their snouts into the steaming mess of skins and spuds and turnips and God knows what, heads down, they grunted and gorged as if they hadn't had a decent feed in months. At first, the smell of the slops had made my stomach heave, but the sight and sound of the brutes appearing to have such utter joy in pigging out, soon overcame my squeamishness.

When we were at our ease with door-keeping at feeding time, we were promoted to cleaning out the sty, which required that we shovel the grey turds that lay about into a wheelbarrow, brush and slosh the floor of the shed with water, and lay down fresh straw. Rather than open the gate of the pig pen, because the pigs were always looking for a chance to dash for freedom, we would climb into the sty with brushes and shovels, cajole the pigs or chase them into their shed and close its door. The pigs safely locked up we could shovel the mess in the sty into a wheelbarrow.

During one chase, a pig jammed Norman against the corner of the fence and wouldn't let him go. We knew not to pull the pig's tail, for the pig would take offence and bite. Two hundred pounds of offended pork could spin with the speed of a whipped spinning-top. And we were nervous about straddling it and pulling it by its ears, as Victor and Jimmy would have done. So Bobby, Herbie and I took hold of its rump to move it sideways and give Norman room to escape. We dug our heels in the dirt and pulled. Without warning the pig moved forward, and with the sudden loss of resistance, we spread-eagled backwards into the clabber. Norman walked away, unharmed, and unmarked, except for clabbered shoes.

We grew fond of the beasts, with their anthropoid eye lashes, their snorts and grunts, and as we became less fearful of them, we would try to ride on them, but they would have none of that, and the aspiring Buffalo Bill would find himself flung on his backside, and having to explain to his mother why his trousers stank of pig clabber. But I think we were fond of them most of all because they loved to be free.

Now and again a hue and cry roused a dozing farmyard: 'Th' pigs are out! Th' pigs are out!' Taking advantage of a carelessly half-closed gate, the pigs would file out of the sty and race straight through a nearby field toward a sheugh, where they wallowed like hippos. It took a while for Victor and Jimmy, with a bit of help from us, to round them up. You had to wade into the sheugh with a stick, whack a pig across the backside, and hope it didn't turn on you but took the hint in the spirit of friendship and climbed out of the mud. You shouted at them, they squealed back, and somehow you broke up the party, like parents who wade into a children's birthday bash that has gotten out of hand. Now and again a stubborn beast had to be roped and hauled up the field like a laggard dog on a leash.

One afternoon, we decided to enter the sty through the gate rather than climb over the fence. A brute of a porker was waiting for us to make this mistake, and timed his dash well. We were taken by surprise, instead of shutting the gate immediately to prevent the others escaping, we turned to catch the pig. The gate was slammed open against the fence with the surge of its mates pouring through in an exodus towards the sheugh. We yelled, 'Th' pigs are out!' And we heard Jinny's voice like an accusing echo, 'Th' boys have let th' pigs out!'

Victor and Jimmy were somewhere well out of earshot of Jinny's cry, if that was possible, and Jinny came wading along in her water boots to direct the round-up. Within minutes, all was chaos and tumult. Without sticks, we leaped into the mud and water to urge the pigs out. Jinny stood at the edge of the sheugh shouting directions to us, we shouted at the pigs, the pigs grunted and squealed in their pleasure. We spluttered and laughed between our gulders, for when we succeeded with shoving a pig out of the mire, it would turn and plunge back into it. It splashed, we splashed, it rolled in the mud, we rolled in the mud trying to wrap our arms around its neck or hind legs while it wiggled and slipped free. Now, it was hard to tell who was wallowing, the pigs or the boys. Only with the arrival of Victor and Jimmy, now alerted by the commotion, did we begin with seriousness to herd the reluctant beasts back to the sty. Wringing wet and splattered with mud, tired, happy with having a good explanation for our filthy state, we squelched back to the farm house. Our mothers stared at us.

'God almighty, wher've youse been?'

'In the sheugh wi' th' pigs. They'd escaped.'

'Is nat hard to see who'd th' most fun. Git them clothes off ye an' git over t'th'pump.'

The water was cold, but it failed to cool our joy.

As the summer mellowed into autumn, it became clear that soon we were going back to Belfast. My father, on one of his rare visits because he worked six-day weeks, brought news that there had been no more air raids on Belfast, and that the Government believed that the Luftwaffe had lost interest in the city because Hitler was now at war with Russia.

A market day fell just a few days before we packed our cases to return home. We heard that some of the pigs would be shipped to market, and we offered our help to Victor and Jimmy, and hoped, though with faint hope, that this time we could go to market, and see the pigs safely to their new owners. But Victor gently rejected our offer. Too dangerous, he said. 'But we know the pigs now,' we protested. Victor was firm. A man had arrived, he said, who would help him move them. Could we see them loaded on to the cart, and follow them up the lane to the road? we asked. At that point, Victor told our mothers that we were to be kept in the house. It was a strange order, because we never expected Victor to behave like this with us. Jinny went further: we were to stay in the kitchen, not go into any of the rooms at the front of the house, not even into our bedroom, until the pigs had left. We could not make sense of all this. We protested to our mothers: 'Th' pigs are only goin' to t'market.'

'Yis. But Jinny's afraid they might break free an' run wild and angry, and hurt one of youse.'

They ushered us into the kitchen, where Jinny laid bread and milk on the table and bade us eat. Shortly afterwards, terrible squeals broke out, followed by the rapid creaks of the farmyard pump. At first, we thought that Victor and Jimmy were washing the pigs, and we said to one another that we could have done that job. Another squeal, then a silence, then a rapid creak of the pump. The awful truth behind Victor's refusal to let us help him dawned on us.

'That man, Mammy. The man that came t'help Victor, th'man we don't know. Who's he?'

Jinny answered:

'Hush now, its all right. Victor can't do it hisself. Nor Jimmy.'

The brutal truth was no consolation, and we wept for the pigs, our pigs. I thought of Jimmy, and drew solace from the fact that he had not wielded the knife.

On our last morning, I gazed out of our bedroom window for a final glimpse of the farm that already held memories I would keep alive by constant repetition among my friends and within our family. The ground around the pump was wet, not from rain, but from an excess of water, and I recalled my first impression of the pump.

Our leave-taking at the bus was as awkward as our meeting. We said thanks and shook hands with Jinny, Victor, and Jimmy. Victor said, 'Luk after yersels.' Jimmy smiled as he had on the day we had first met. He and I had never conversed in all the weeks that had passed, and while I still thought he was bemused by us, I knew, indeed, had known all along, that he had been too shy to talk to us.

The streets of Belfast were grey and narrow, and although cleared of rubble, bore the scars of the blitz. Our house seemed forlorn and small, its rooms cramped. After the long journey, I slept soundly. Late in the morning, I awakened expecting to see the sun already high in the sky, impatient for me to get dressed and out into the fields, but it wasn't there. The sky was pale and featureless. When I took to the street, I heard a shout:

'Hey, Willie, you're home.'

I was. And I wasn't. I was thinking: it must have rained some time in Lough-gilly. How else would apple trees blossom, and a sheugh fill with water?

Epilogue

Many years passed before I saw Jinny and Victor Hale again. My brother had learned that they had retired, and had moved into Belfast after selling the farm, and he organised a little reunion. In the warmth of a cosy parlour, the Hales welcomed us, Herbie, Vi, Norman and me, as 'the visitors', and marvelled how we had grown and how changed. But within minutes we were evacuees again. Jinny served us tea and apple pie. No treat could have matched it, for it was as chock full of memories, as it was of goodness.

'Apples from th' farm, Jinny?'

'Ach, no,' Jinny replied.

'Then it's th' touch, Jinny, not just what's in th' pie. I've yet to taste a better apple pie.'

Everyone concurred, and Jinny blushed with pleasure to the sole of her carpet slippers, and as if to ward off further praise she said:

'After ye left, I wis luking around in yer bedroom, doin' a bit of tidyin', and I noticed th' sag in th'canopy over th'bed. So, I stud on a cheair an' luked fer the cause, an' there in th'middle of th'canopy was a bushel o' dried-up apple butts, an' I says to meself, 'Them boys, them bad, bad boys'.'

We roared.

'Now ye know, Jinny, why we didn't mind being sent to our room without our tea as a punishment. We had stashed apples under the bed, behind th' po.'

Jinny lifted her arms, and let them fall into her lap.

'Away wi' ye. I hope yer nat bad boys still,' she said.

Then one of us asked her the most important question:

'Jinny, why did you take seven evacuees when you only asked for one?'

She answered, waving her long thin ageing hands as if to halt any effusion of gratitude.

'Och, I culdn't say no, an' sure, ye were no trouble at' all.'

Chapter 9

THE BACK FIELD

THE 'BACK field', as it was known in the neighbourhood to distinguish it from the fields that swept from the top of our street up the hillside toward the Horseshoe Road, was an acre or two of grassy ground, irregular in shape, between the back of our houses and the houseless Berwick Road. It looked like a meadow surrendered by a slothful farmer to the willfulness of nature.

In season, crowds of dandelions (known locally as 'pee-the-beds') revelled in their brief existence from bud to puffball; scatterings of buttercups swayed drunkenly in the breezes; and colonies of daisies and clover quietly hugged the earth, holding their own against encroaching tussocks of coarse grass and clumps of docken and bulrushes. Common nettles, whose leaves would leave burning welts on the hapless legs of girls in frocks and boys in short trousers who brushed against them, flourished innocently among the tall grasses that pressed against the crooked line of fences demarcating the small gardens from field. Thistles concealed themselves in tussocks.

Here and there the greensward was poxed with small square claybrown craters left by desultory gardeners who had peeled back the sod to dig out and riddle the topsoil for their small gardens. At times, heavy rainfalls transformed the craters into mud holes, and so the field was quite useless for football and cricket.

This state of natural anarchy encouraged slovenly people to dump rubbish on one end of it: stained mattresses with the hair and straw stuffing spilling from gashes in the fabric, rusty bedsprings, smashed chairs, bits of splintered floorboards or door jambs, sodden lumps of lath and plaster, empty paint tins, and, sometimes, a sack of drowned kittens.

From time to time – that is, months apart in time, maybe years – the bin men, at the bidding of the health authorities, I suppose, carted away the debris.

The rains took care of dirt left by dogs, and by boys caught short on the way home from school, and someone always would bury the dead kittens.

The city council appeared to have abandoned the field, and so we, the children of the nearby streets, claimed it for our own. We avoided, if we were careful, the nettles and shit and we ignored the dead kittens after we sanitised them with our chant:

'No fever in our house, one, two, three.'

This was followed by a spit, or two to ward off a disease worse than scarlet fever. Our house was one of many whose back overlooked the field, and from the scullery window or back door, my mother could observe her children playing there, if she had a mind to. We were safer there, she thought, than walking to the public playgrounds in other parts of the city.

'Wher'ye goin'?' she would ask me, as I squeezed past her in our narrow scullery.

'Out in th' back field, Mammy.'

'Don't get your feet wet. An' mind them nettles. I don't want ye comin' in here whingeing with welts on yer legs. An' don't bring dog's dirt in on yer shoes.'

'No, Mammy. Yes, Mammy. No, Mammy.'

We did, we didn't, we did, at times. Not that we intended to. Once into the field, we were heedless of warnings and oblivious of any eye observing us from a scullery or upstairs bedroom window.

Only the swings took me to city playgrounds, the cold smooth feel of the chain, even on a hot day, and the hypnotic creak and scrape of the bolts in the flanges of the top bar as the swing rose and fell and rose again, pushing upward through the air toward heaven before falling back to earth. The thrill of soaring on a swing beat a quick shoot down a slide, which anyway was often sticky from wet knickers or trousers. I had no truck with merry-go-rounds which made me dizzy and sick, or sand pits dampened down with toddlers' wee. The seesaws were tame, unless you stood on them instead of sitting. But on a swing you could pump yourself so high that had you let go you believed you would have sailed over the high railings and landed among rooks on tree tops, or into the bleach works dam beyond the trees, and drowned. The nearest playground was at least half an hour's walk from our street. It occupied a corner of a beautiful parkland of rolling greensward and stands of chestnut, beech and sycamore trees. The park had lost its perimeter of iron railings to the war effort, but the playground remained enclosed within a high wire fence.

A grumpy 'parkie' patrolled its precincts, and would appear out of nowhere like a phantom in a film, blowing his peeler's whistle until he was blue in the face, waving his walking stick like a sword, and shouting at some miscreant swinging wildly or climbing up the slide or spinning the merry-go-round at breakneck speed or standing on the seesaw. As the first shades of dusk settled on the park, a long high liquid trill of his whistle, which brought forth a raucous riposte from the crows in the treetops, signalled the closing of the playground. Brandishing his walking stick, he rounded up stragglers who lingered over their last minutes of pleasure, and ushered everyone out through the huge iron gate into the street. Satisfied that nobody remained among the dying swings or hidden behind the motionless merry-go-round, he locked the gate. Every night, every Sunday, every Christmas Day, behind the barred gate the playground lay silent and still and forlorn, a microcosm of a world without children.

The back field had no swings, but neither was it fenced by iron railings nor policed by a parkie. Only the occasional apparition of a wandering, bored 'peeler', who might think we were delinquents, threatened our games. It lay freely at hand to us every hour of the day and night, every day of the year, and in all weathers, for whatever our imaginations could devise.

But most of all, the back field was the place for fires. Not wild fires set by willful youths, but purposeful fires, wee fires that bonded a gang of boys into a memory of years when children were free to be children.

I

All our houses had fireplaces in the kitchen that doubled as a living-room, and so I knew how to light a fire in the grate using kindling my mother usually bought from a street vendor, a fellow in an unkempt unbuttoned gabardine and a warped duncher, who did the rounds of the streets pushing a handcart loaded with bundles of sticks and shouting from time to time in a lilting hoarse voice: 'Sticks! Thruppence a bunnel.' Sometimes boys peddled kindling piled in small carts made of apple boxes and pram wheels.

I fancied doing the same thing to make some money for fish and chips and a night at the pictures, but never did. I once earned thruppence from my mother for chopping kindling from some old boards I had found in the back field, but it cost me a split nail in the index finger of my right hand. Being left-handed, I had held a board end up with my right hand, not paying attention to where my fingers were placed, and brought the hatchet down on the top third of one finger, splitting it wide open. Forever after, two finger nails grew where only one had the right to be.

Lighting a fire at home was a chore. We didn't have two-handed bellows, and if the coals on top of the sticks didn't turn red before the sticks burned down, you put the coal shovel up against the grate and covered it and the fireplace opening with a sheet of newspaper. The draught sucked the sheet of paper into a concave like a kite caught in the wind. Air would roar up the chimney, and in a minute or two the coals would be red-hot. You watched the paper, and from time to time, touched it, for if it got too hot, it would turn yellow and burst into flames. Then you had to be quick at shoving it into the fire.

Sometimes the draught sucked the burning paper up the flue and set the chimney on fire, and you would run out of the house to see if thick black smoke poured and roared from the chimney, and if flakes of burning paper and soot spiralled into the sky. If so, the chimney was on fire, and you ran up the stairs to feel the bedroom wall behind which the flue ran, to see if it was hot. If it wasn't, you knew that the chimney fire would soon burn out, at which time lumps of hot soot usually fell down the flue into the grate and spewed soot all over the kitchen, the sofa and chairs, the clock and ornaments on the mantelpiece, and the wireless set. If the wall was hot, you just about wet your trousers because your house was in danger of catching fire. Some people deliberately set fire to their chimneys to burn out the soot that was blocking the draught needed to draw the fire. It saved them having to hire one of the soot-caked chimney sweeps who stalked the streets looking for business, and it kept the fire brigades on their toes.

Apart from the heady cocktail of anxiety and excitement I tasted on the few occasions I did set the flue ablaze but without burning the house down, stoking the grate at home was too routine to give pleasure. A wood fire in the back field appealed to me in a way a coal fire in the kitchen could not. Hunkered at a wee blaze, I was a lonesome cowboy or an explorer or whomsoever my fancy summoned from the books and weekly comics I had been reading. Mostly, I was just myself, wrapped in the fire's warmth.

'Can I have a match, Mammy?'

'What for?'

'We wanna light a fire in th' back field.'

'Who's 'we'?'

'Ye know. Our gang. Me an' Norman. Herbie. Ernie. Charlie. Jim an' Cecil might come too.'

Mothers always wanted to be told what company you kept, even though they already knew. Roughly of the same age, we all lived within spitting or shouting distance of each other on the same street. We were good mates most of the time, and shared the same territorial and class bond. Satisfied that this company was no danger to my body or morals, my mother handed me a few matches in a matchbox:

'Mind you don't burn yourselves, nigh. An' bring me the box back.'

For a minute or two she would watch from the yard door while we gathered bits of paper and sticks from the rubbish heaps for a wee fire, and then would turn back to her tin bath full of hot washing and bend her head into the rising steam. Glancing toward the house, I would notice her arms pumping up and down the washboard. Or if the scrubbing was done, she would be turning the handle of the mangle with one hand while catching the flattened cardboard-stiff white sheets and shirts with the other, a job I sometimes helped her with until my arms wearied.

Grand it was, especially at dusk, to squat at a wee fire with your mates and warm your hands and shins, and if the air was frigid, turn your back to the heat. Nobody paid attention to jerseys ravelling at the cuffs or at the elbows or around the waist or all over, or to patches in the arse of trousers, or to the grey cardboard visible on the frayed peaks of skull caps, or to holes in shoes, or that somebody from time to time wiped his nose on his sleeve. Sometimes, in silence you watched the seductive dancing of flames along bits of broken boards gathered from the field and bombed-out houses, and listened to the crackle of burning wood. Or you picked at the dirtpurple scabs on your bare knees and shins, half-expecting to find underneath the white sheen of bone.

But it was grander to smoke at the fire. You never believed the lie you were told, that cigarettes would stunt your growth; you saw tall smokers, and your own father, who was neither tall nor small, smoked and wasn't stunted. The thing you feared was nicotine fingers, because they gave you away, and my mother, who could put the fear of God into me, had warned me that I was never to put a cigarette in my mouth.

Just a month short of my eighth birthday I had my first smoke sitting at a wee fire in the back field with my brother and Herbie. Our fegs were tea leaves filched from mother's tea caddy, and rolled in small bits of newspaper. At our first attempt, the paper caught fire and singed our eyelashes. A second attempt was more successful, but all we inhaled was the acrid odour of burnt paper. Disappointed, we tried the pulp of bulrushes, but it wouldn't smoulder.

Then we heard from a boy at school that you could smoke a cinnamon stick. We pooled our pennies and bought a couple. They were sold in chemist shops, and the chemist believed you wanted them to chew for the good of your health. You broke a stick in half, because the shorter the stick the better the draw, lit the end in the fire, waved it until it glowed, stuck it in your mouth and sucked hard because the smoke was difficult to draw down the stick. It frequently went out, but you didn't mind; you were smoking and your fingers didn't stain a telltale yellow. Besides, these fegs had one advantage over the real thing; total consumption. When you tired of smoking, or felt your cheeks about to collapse into permanent concaves from having to draw arduously to get a wafer of smoke, you could eat the stick. Nobody in his right mind would eat the butt of a Woodbine.

And so, having solved the problem of what to smoke, we sat at our wee fires, puffed or chewed our cinnamon fegs, and, with a clear conscience and no anxiety, talked like the decent Irishmen we were.

Most often, our talk around the fire was desultory; about school and canings, gangs and fights, films and football, and the war. If anyone had seen a film the rest of us had missed, we always asked, 'Who was the wee man?' If it didn't have one, we concluded it wasn't worth watching, and if it did, we would compare him to Roy Rogers' side-kick, Gabby Hayes, or Windy Halliday, as he was known. For no 'wee man', we all nodded in agreement, could match his wild-eyed joyous pursuit of outlaws nor the power and distance of his tobacco-fuelled spit.

We argued about almost everything, and when arguments degenerated into name-calling and our tempers unravelled, up went our fists. As we nudged puberty, we bantered each other about the girls we fancied, or who fancied us. In lighter moods we tested our punning skill with 'Knock, knock. Who's there', tittered over a mix of the corn reaped from comics and wisecracks picked up from 'The Dead End Kids', and sniggered at the double-entendres we thought we had heard, but in fact, scarcely understood, on the wireless. *ITMA* (Tommy Handley and his gang in 'It's That Man Again') was the most popular wartime comedy on the wireless. Then someone would tell a joke about bowels and bogs, and we would convulse with laughter.

From time to time, we made fire with the aid of a spectacles' lens, which drew the sun's rays to a burning tip at the bottom of a small heap of dry grass. But sunshine and tinder dry grass were not often handy most of the year. At pictures in the cinema about the olden days, we saw soldiers light the fuse on a barrel of gunpowder by striking two flints together, but when we aped them with a pair of flint stones my brother and I had picked up at Carnmoney graveyard on a visit to Grandma's grave, we made lots of sparks but no fire.

Once we tried to light a fire the way Herbie and I had seen it done at a Wolf Cub meeting. With my penknife, I rounded a stick while Herbie gouged a thimble-sized hollow in a piece of wood. Herbie took the first turn. He placed the stick in the hollow, and using the palms of his hands, twirled it quickly back and forth. We watched for the first whiff of smoke which would tell us the stick was about to smoulder. Herbie twirled and twirled until his hands tired. No smoke. I took over. Our patience began to drain.

'Rub, Willie. Yer nat twirling fast enough.'

'I am so. Me hans is gittin' blisters.'

'Yer nat holdin' the stick straight enough.'

'I am so. It's youse that's cockeyed.'

Cecil took over. Then Ernie. When a thread of smoke finally appeared, someone shoved a handful of dry grass against the stick, and we all blew, and blew, but nothing happened. Not a flicker of flame, not even a sliver of ember, and the thin feather of smoke disappeared into the air. It was plain to me that it would be easier to cadge matches from Mammy.

During the war years, boys collected brass cap badges and uniform buttons of regiments in the British Army. I had some I guarded carefully, along with bits of bomb shrapnel from the Blitzes and a few empty .303 bullet cartridges, because I believed that having a regimental badge was the next best thing to wearing a uniform. Besides, as with stamps or coin collections, at school there was a market for badges and you could get thruppence for a decent lead replica. So, with Herbie and Norman, I went into the smelting and casting business.

We scoured blitzed houses in the neighbourhood for short pieces of lead pipe, and ripped stretches of lead flashing from the flat roofs of the bomb-damaged shops at the bottom of the street. To our pile of pilfered lead we added toy lead soldiers discharged from active duty, either because they had been dismembered, decapitated, or had simply lost their uniforms of paint, which tended to wear off with much handling.

With matches I had snitched from a shelf above the gas stove in our scullery, because I didn't want my mother to know I was smelting lead, since that admission would lead to questions about where the lead came from, followed by her dire predictions that I would end up in a home for bad boys, we set the fire going in a shallow pit. While the sticks burned, we dug pieces of red clay from a hole in the field, kneaded them in our hands with spit until they were the texture of putty, and made a number of small clay tablets, on which we imprinted the images of badges and buttons.

When the fire was hot enough we set an empty floor polish tin on the embers and dropped bits of dirty grey lead into it. The lead slowly melted into a silver puddle flecked with dirty streaks. Now and again, we dropped a lead soldier into the tin, and watched it dissolve into the molten lead like an exhausted swimmer sinking beneath the sea. Gingerly lifting the tin from the fire with a pair of pliers I had borrowed from my father's shoe repair box – we didn't wear gloves – we took turns at carefully pouring the hot bright liquid into the clay moulds. When the lead had set, we pried the replica from its clay bed and tossed it on the grass. Some came out marred; others near perfect. With a small narrow file, we buffed away excess lead from the edges of the badges until we were satisfied with our work. The marred replicas went back into the tin for a second try.

Holding a warm replica in my hand, and admiring its argent resemblance to the real thing, I always felt pleased with myself in a way that was quite different from the pleasure of getting high marks for algebra or spelling at school, or even from scoring a goal in football or hitting a six in street cricket. I had made a thing of beauty, at least in my eyes. And, besides, at school a good replica should fetch enough money for a parcel of hot chips or even the price of a matinee at the Forum or Park picture houses.

Our wee fires were a source of something else. Something to eat. A tin of beans tasted and smelled better cooked on the fires outside than on a gas stove, even if you almost roasted the skin of your fingers holding the tin while one of your mates ripped it open with a penknife or your father's screwdriver. You could imagine yourself to be a cowboy, particularly a baddie like Billy the Kid. But beans were a rare treat because you had to cadge your mother for a tin. Not so with potatoes.

In those austere wartime years of food rationing, potatoes were plentiful. We grew them in our small back garden, when my father would take the notion to plant the seedlings in the spring. He often said spuds were better for us than the fancy foods the rich ate. He said it with such authority that I didn't doubt him. I reasoned, Daddy was a St John Ambulance man and he must have learned this fact from the doctors who taught him First Aid. After all, potatoes were treated with respect. We knew about the potato famine, how millions of Irish had perished a hundred years earlier when the potato crops failed and how wee children had died with green mouths in ditches alongside fields full of turnips.

At home, when the ration coupons for dried eggs and meat were used up and my mother's purse just about empty, we ate 'champ', mashed spuds mixed with chopped scallions, a dinner you could mess about with for a minute without your mother barging you to stop playing with your food, for she knew that in time you wouldn't leave a trace of spud on the plate. You heaped the hot mash on the plate, smoothed it into a miniature green-flecked Mount Fuji, dropped a lump of butter or margarine into a spoon-sized crater you had made on its top, and as the butter melted, you gently opened the crater to let the golden lava stream down the spuddy slopes. We had it often, and never tired of it. But Mammy never baked the potatoes. By a happy accident at one of our fires, I learned how to do that myself.

At first, I used to cook the spuds in a big fire, thinking that the bigger the fire the better and quicker they would cook. But they burned and the black cinder skin tasted worse than burnt toast, and the uncooked fibre underneath felt and tasted like candle grease, and I would have to pretend I had a good feast.

Raking though the ashes of a dying fire after a cookout, Norman and I found a spud we had overlooked, because it had been buried in the ashes. The skin was dark but not burnt black, and its fibre was tender. We had hit on the secret of baking potatoes. Lots of hot ash, and – this was the hardest part – patience. But it was always worth the waiting.

'Would you give me a spud an' a poke of salt, Mammy?'
'What for?'
'We're goin' to cook spuds in the fire. Would ye want one, Mammy?'
'It would only give me indigestion.'
'But we know how to cook spuds soft. Honest, we do, Mammy.'
'Away ye go. Mind ye don't burn yourselves.'
'We won't, Mammy.'

We didn't. Ever. Except for a burn or two on our jerseys from a spark but that didn't really count. On a winter's day in the back field, a cold north wind pinches your cheeks and ears and wraps around your bare knees, raising goose pimples on your thighs. Your nose drips like a slow leak. But you don't notice these things much, because seated at a warm fire, you're biting into the crisp skin of a hot spud. Musty steam fills your nose and fans out into the cold air. You sprinkle salt from a little paper poke on the hot white flesh, bite again and roll the soft hot lump around your mouth until it is cool enough to chew and swallow.

If hungry Adam had among the exotic fruits of the Garden of Eden such a pleasure it might have taken his mind off that fatal fruit, the source, the theologians say, of all our misery.

Chapter 10

GREEN GRAVEL

I

In spring and summer the field dressed itself, in spite of nettles and bulrushes and rubbish, with daisies, dandelions, buttercups, and clover. Other flowers grew unnoticed, here and there tufted vetch, or a lone small family of primroses.

The flowers drew girls to the field, and sometimes we would drift toward them, to sit nearby and make daisy chains fit for dainty wrists and ankles, or into a garland for the Queen of the May. We would strip the small white petals off a daisy to the beat of 'She loves me, she loves me not,' and feel a twinge of pleasure when the last petal matched a secret desire, or blushed when our partner loudly and facetiously proclaimed an affirmative. Holding a buttercup under a chin, we looked for the yellow reflection that betrayed a fondness for butter, and then questioned the evidence. With the juice of the stems of dandelions, we tattooed the backs of our hands and wrists with small ovals, and then worried about peeing the bed that night.

Girls rarely joined us at our autumn and winter fires, and when they did we worried that their frocks might catch a flame. A common cautionary tale in those days was the tragedy of the girl, who in her long frock or nightie stood too close to the kitchen grate and was burned to death. And most of us had sisters. Yet we didn't mind, on a spring or summer evening, when a girl called to us as we lazed on the grass, to join her and her mates in 'The Farmer's in the Dell' or 'Down on the Carpet'. Responding to some indistinct need, we were anxious to hold hands with girls and so, hand in hand we circled to the girls' airy emphatic singing.

As the game progressed, you became anxious to be chosen by the girl you fancied. If you were not, you felt it, and if someone you didn't fancy chose you, you scringed your teeth and put up with it. For then you knew, and others too, who fancied whom, and afterwards, when the games ended and the girls departed, the slagging would begin, out of jealousy or spite or sheer bloody-mindedness. If it didn't end in a fight among us, it left us at odds with one another. And in the twilight you slunk from the field to your house and to the comfort of *The Hotspur* or *The Champion* comic.

One game always left me melancholy. It required no pairing of partners, no blushing choices, and never ended in a quarrel. It was not really a game, but a circle song, usually sung by girls. They would call to us to join their circle, but most often we preferred to loll on the grass and watch the frocks go by.

At first, the girls' voices are bright, ethereal, the rhythm of the lines assured:

> *Green gravel, green gravel,*
> *Your grass is so green,*
> *You're the fairest young damsel*
> *I ev-er have seen.*

They circle slowly, their heads up, their faces expressionless; their eyes flitting around the circle:

> *I washed her, I dressed her,*
> *I clothed her in silk,*
> *And I wrote down her name*
> *With a glass pen and ink.*

Then, as the song enters its tragic phase, the turning circle slows to a funereal pace, the voices rise and fall dolefully, and the girls lower their heads until they are gazing at a spot in the centre of the circle, a ring of daisies, perhaps:

> *O Kathleen, O Kathleen,*
> *Your true love is dead*
> *I sent you a letter*
> *To turn back your head.*

At the last word of the song the circle comes to rest. The silence and stillness are held for a moment. Then the circle breaks, the girls scatter, and I am left wondering why a sadness has seeped into my bones, like a chill from a cold small rain. In the distance I hear my mother's voice calling me home for tea.

II

With the coming of summer the back field became the theatre for our wild fantasies. Our inspiration came from the films we saw at the Forum, the Park, the Crumlin, the Stadium (a flea-pit), the Lyceum, the Capitol. With Herbie and my brother, I went to the Saturday matinees as religiously as to Sunday school. After a film that had wholly captivated us, kidneys and all, for eighty or ninety minutes, we would gather our gang in the back field, and transform it into a Hollywood back lot. And until darkness fell we played, and replayed, the scenes that had enthralled us.

We argued over who would be Apaches, and who the cowboys or Cavalry. The casting was rarely amicable, for each of us had an image of himself as a hero and none of us wanted to be the baddie. But, since the baddies were always killed, if you fancied yourself to be good at dying, the part was yours for the asking. And so, the barneys were brief, and nobody felt hurt.

Action! Roll the camera.

The sun is casting long shadows. An Apache in a jersey lies behind a tussock. A feather, maybe a pigeon's or a crow's or better still a seagull's picked up at Helen's Bay, tied firmly by a ribbon or length of wool, sticks up aslant at the back of his head. He grips an ash bow strung with cord and arrows of willow tipped with chicken wire. Yards away kneels Wild Bill Hickock, wearing a misshapen paddy hat too big for his small head. He aims a wooden rifle carved from a piece of scrap wood, because you can't buy a metal gun in a shop in these days, and so you do your best with what you have, and don't girn about it. Under the scorching desert sun they shoot, bullets whining. 'Got ya'. 'No, ye didn't'. 'Yis, I did'. 'No, ye didn't. I was kilt last time'. 'Alright', and the loser twists and turns and bends and groans in fake agony, and, if brave enough, pitches himself on the turf, and rolls over on his back, eyes shut tight against the bluegold light. And as his chums praise his dying fall, he feels gloriously alive.

Summer rain clouds hang low in the sky. A handful of small knights without armour, except for bin lids held close to their chests, in bare knees and socks around their ankles, charge down the soggy field brandishing swords split from old boards, and yelling in a tongue known only to God or the devil. They clash with their foe, bin lid against bin lid, sword against sword. Yells become yelps as cardboard hand-guards on the swords crumple under the blows, or a bin lid bangs a brow. The battle is brief, for someone has whimpered: 'Ye don't need to hit so hard,' and recriminations have broken out. Under a lowering sky, the warriors wipe their noses and nurse their bruised knuckles, and drag their swords and bin lids and sodstained arses toward home and a warm hearth.

Galleons commandeer the blue ocean overhead. Pirates capped in their mothers' old head scarves, and their socks around their ankles, clash on the bloody deck of *The Seahawk*. The mélée soon sorts itself into a circle, for the main attraction is the duel between Errol Flynn without the moustache, and the villainous Basil Rathbone without his beard. It is a duel to the death, or until one sword breaks, which is bound to happen sooner or later, and then a real fight will begin, which will take you back to the argument about who had wanted to be Errol Flynn and who thought himself best at slowly dying from a sword thrust to the belly.

But battles long ago were not uppermost in our minds. A real war, not a Hollywood fantasy, was taking place, and it had come home to us in the Blitz. We sat by the wireless at nine o'clock at night to hear the BBC tell us of battles in Italy and Russia and air-raids over England and Germany. Winston Churchill told us of D-Day, of the greatest armada in history, and we crossed our fingers, said our prayers, and carried the conflict into the back field, as if by mimicking war ourselves, we might by sympathetic magic ensure the defeat of Hitler and the Nazis.

As much as possible, you dressed for battle. Boots, if you had them, rather than shoes, for soldiers wore boots. Belt around your lumber jacket. Whatever suitable headgear you could find at home. Here I was lucky. Plundering one afternoon in a big trunk behind the wardrobe in our house, I found a steel helmet, peaked field cap with chin-strap, and Sam Browne belt. They belonged to a great-uncle who had seen service in the Great War and in India. I wore the helmet precariously on my small head, for it had a tendency to slip over my eyes and put me off my aim, but I was determined not to go to war without it. Once, as I fell into a trench, the helmet tipped forward and its rim caught me across the nose, drawing blood. Afterwards, I wore the peaked cap with the chin strap, and carried the tin hat mainly for effect. But when I was hunkered in a wee foxhole as clay pellets rained down, I reached for it.

When we had enough boys for a war, we divided into an even number of Germans and British soldiers. Nobody wanted to be Jerries, but usually after much arguing the matter was settled because you can't have a battle without two armies. After another argy-bargy about who would occupy which of the two trenches we had dug over time by deepening the various mud holes left by erstwhile gardeners, we set about making clay bullets and hand grenades from the brown and yellow clay of the trench. We hunkered down, and at the shout of 'Fire' – the shouter also the subject of an argy-bargy between claimants to the privilege – we hurled the bullets and grenades at each other until we had expended all the ammunition; whereupon we called a truce to gather up the pellets that had fallen between and in the trenches. We threw until our arms tired, or until we were fed up with arguing about who was winning.

Not all battles ended as we had planned. The 'Germans', who were supposed to lose, sometimes won, and somebody would be annoyed about that. If you were hit you were supposed to lie down and stop throwing, but some boys had a remarkable ability to come back to life with a vengeance. Occasionally, an eejit stuck his head up too high and took a pellet in the face. He would accuse his 'enemy' of meaning to hit him there, and the battle would end in a fist-fight. After that, we would abandon the field, and go home to listen to the wireless for news of the real war.

Epilogue

Two years after the war ended, most of us left school to work in factories
or mills, shops or the shipyard, and we had no time to spend in the field. It
became merely a short cut on our journeys to and from work, and I would
cross it indifferent to the ashes of burnt out fires and the narrow trenches
now filling in with fresh sod. When houses were built along the Berwick
Road perimeter, the field shrunk to a small enclosure. Children ceased to
play there, and as if in grief, the field became an unsightly mass of long
tangled grasses and bulrushes.

   And human nature also took its own course. As we grew up – Herbie,
Bobby, Charlie, Ernie, Cecil, Jim, Norman, and me – the bonds that had
united our gang in the back field weakened, and all too soon, except for
their traces in memory, dissolved.

Chapter 11

MY FATHER'S CARBUNCLE

SOMETIMES MY father was a pain in the neck, as far as my mother was concerned. He was a heavy smoker, and from time to time he ran out of cigarettes by Thursday, and had no money to buy any until payday. By midweek too, my mother had little left from the housekeeping allowance he had given her on the previous Friday from his labourer's pay packet, and even if she might have been able to hand over a shilling or two to him for ten Woodbines, she wouldn't, because food on the table for her children came before any other contingency. And she didn't smoke.

Without a cigarette to sustain him, except the odd one he got at work from a sympathetic workmate, my father was misery itself. In the evenings after tea time, he would sit for a minute with the evening paper *The Belfast Telegraph*, sigh, moan about not having a cigarette, get up and pace back and forth between the kitchen and the scullery, and between the scullery and the back yard. Usually, he was an easy-going man, but at any sharp word from my mother – and she was not slow to chide him for his restlessness: 'For God's sake Billy, will ye sit down or go out' – an argy-bargy would erupt. They would step into the scullery. My brother, sisters and I would exchange glance and grimaces, as we overheard them trade curses behind the closed scullery door, their voices rising until the yard door slammed when father took himself out into the back garden. The scullery door would open, and mother would stride through the kitchen, lift her coat off a peg in the hallway, and leave, without a word to us, for a short walk around the nearby Berwick Road. And the front door would slam. Within half an hour they would be back in the house, but neither would speak to the other the rest of the evening.

After one too many of these rows, my mother devised a little stratagem to ward off future aggravations of this kind. Early in the week, she bought from what was left of the housekeeping money a packet of five Woodbines or ten Players cigarettes, whatever she could afford, and hid it. When my father's yen for a feg had him walking around the house as if he was afraid to sit down, and had him sighing as though all the world's troubles had settled on his shoulders, she would hand him a couple of cigarettes, and he would sigh like a man reprieved from a life sentence in the Crumlin Jail.

Over time, however, he began to rely on her generous forethought, and she reacted by keeping him in suspense. Come Thursday, he would shyly ask if she had any cigarettes. If she had, sometimes she would deny it, to let him stew for a while, and then relent. But if she hadn't, and he thought she had, he wouldn't accept her denials. That kicked off a slagging match; off to the scullery they would go, the back door would bang, and our mother would make another circuit of the Berwick.

One evening, my father's restlessness had a different and rather ominous source. He had a pain in his neck. Mother took a look at it and gave him the bad news. What looked like a small round boil had taken root on his nape. By its colour and hardness, it looked as if a microbe had decided to dig itself in 'for the duration', as we used to say. Some years earlier my father had been tortured by boils, and when he spoke of it, he added, 'Nivir agane.' But nature is deaf to our entreaties, and this time he would have one he would 'nivir' forget.

A boil began life as a shillcorn, some said a blackhead, that wouldn't go away when squeezed. Soon you had a crater in your neck the size of a sixpence, or if you were unlucky, the size of a shilling. In my boyhood, this infection was so common among men and boys that you didn't wonder whether you would get a boil but rather *when* you would. You hoped it would happen sooner than later so that you could get it over with, and somehow, it was believed, be immune to them later in life, or if not, at least somewhat inured to the pain.

Everyone in those days thought he knew what caused them: a deficiency of iron in the blood; an excess of grease in the blood. God knows, that was plausible for we consumed animal fat by the pound in soda farls fried in a sea of bacon fat, fish and chips cooked in pure lard, sausages rolling in their own juice, lamb chops cleaned to the white of the bone. My father ate these foods with relish. He was never content at the dinner table, my mother used to say, unless grease was running from his fingertips to his elbows. Some believed that the culprit was bad nerves, and that too might have been plausible in our father's case, since without cigarettes he was fit to be tied; others blamed the soot that fell on the city from chimney smoke and lodged in your pores. We speculated on the cause of our father's boil, none of us quite believing any of these theories, and each of us blaming him somehow for his own misfortune.

A year or so earlier, I had had a boil on my neck, and so I had some idea of what my father was about to go through; the pain of having the boil squeezed and the hot poultice applied to the tender flesh around the angry crater. The anticipation of agony as bad as the agony itself, your head bent forward in readiness for the squeezing, and after that, the eternity while the poultice, a thick layer of hot Kaolin, was smeared on a piece of muslin, before it was laid on the boil. No matter how determined I was to bear the pain without a murmur, like a good soldier, I always hit the ceiling with high dohs worthy of a boy soprano.

Two sessions of this torture a day for a week or so usually routed the microbe from its den, and the cavity would close, leaving the site of the carnage looking as pure as an angel's cheek, so my mother said of mine. For a while, you sported a tiny hollow in your nape that you could feel with a finger tip, and you thought that perhaps you should live a cleaner life, whatever that meant.

As a boy, for some vague reason you felt slightly ashamed to have a boil on your neck. You wondered if that well-dressed woman, sitting opposite you in the tram, noticed it and the telltale forward angle of your head, and was thinking to herself that you must live in a dirty house or that your mother wasn't feeding you vegetables. When you met a neighbour on the street, you would raise your head sharply, whereupon a white-hot pain, like hot needle thrust into a tender nerve, shot up the back of your neck, causing you to jerk your head forward like a rooster. And you were sure that as, in passing he nodded in sympathy, he muttered also, 'Dirty wee fella.'

My boil arrived about the time wooden clogs came on the market to make up for the wartime shortage of shoes because leather was needed for soldiers' boots, I suppose. My mother had bought me a pair, partly, I think, out of sympathy for me. After my boil had been squeezed, cleaned, poulticed and bandaged, I sat rigidly on the sofa like a well-mannered boy holding intestinal gas in check, my head tilted forward as if it had been screwed to my shoulders by a boozy boilermaker and might topple off if I shifted my torso ever so slightly.

I loved the clogs, the loud clack of their contact with the pavement. I loved them too, because they were the footwear of a boy hero in old Holland, who saved a city full of people by plugging the leaking dyke with his finger until he died from exhaustion. Moreover, no boy on our street wore them, and that made me feel, if not quite heroic, at least interestingly different.

The clogs differed from their Dutch cousins in that their uppers were nailed to the wooden soles, and laced they held your foot firmly in the clog. You had to learn to walk in them because the soles, curving up toward the toes, were shod with strips of metal like tiny railway lines and you could skid backwards, if you didn't put your foot down at the right angle on the pavement.

There I go along the street, head thrust forward to keep my boil from contact with the collar of my coat, walking like the docker from down the street coming home drunk in his hobnailed boots on Friday night. I feel myself tilting backwards, so I straighten my head to recover my balance. At that moment, an arrow of pain pierces my neck. In reaction, I pitch forward, the clogs skid under me on their railway lines, forcing me to save myself from bashing my face on the pavement by straightening up sharply again, at which motion my boil again whacks against my coat collar. I see electric sparks leaping from a dislodged tramcar trolley although there is no tram in sight. I am almost insensible. But I stay on my feet. And wonder if the little Dutch boy would have been able to stay so long at the dyke if he had had a boil on his neck.

By the time my boil ran its vindictive course, and the stiffness had gone from my neck, I was walking in my clogs like a dancer in pumps at the Plaza Ballroom, or at least, like a boy in Holland.

We watched with curiosity the small boil on our father's neck grow into a livid lump, a purplish hillock on a red plain. Our mother observed its progress – and our father's increasing distress – with justifiable apprehension, as it turned out. When a sickly yellow head appeared on the lump, it was clear that the 'thing' could not be allowed to get any bigger. It had to be squeezed; otherwise, blood poisoning would set in, and blood poisoning, we knew, could be fatal.

My father sat in a chair, head bent forward. Mother stood behind him, and we crowded around her to watch. On the scullery stove a tin of Kaolin, a white clay manufactured into a paste, rattled in a pot of bubbling water, its strong antiseptic odour filling the kitchen with the smell of a hospital clinic. The clay poultice was believed to be more effective at drawing the poison from the roots of an infection than hot, soggy bread, although in a pinch, bread was better than nothing at all.

He winced and hissed as my mother pierced the skin of the boil with a darning needle sterilised in boiling water, and applied her fingers as gently as she could to his neck, squeezing the yellow pus from the cavity and wiping it clean with cotton wool. Sometimes he moaned 'Aisy, Mabel, aisy,' and my mother, who must have been feeling both the pain and the strain answered 'Keep still, Billy. I'm trying to be as aisy as I can, but if ye keep moving your neck it's only the worse for ye.' We watched silently, our faces contorted in disgust at the sight of the suppurating matter, our teeth scrunching and bodies stiffening in empathy with father's every hiss and wince. Then, while our mother prepared the poultice, my sisters, brother and I took turns to inspect the hole in our father's neck, each of us marvelling at its bloody symmetrical ugliness.

As day after day, my mother laid the hot poultice on my father's neck, it became clear that the infection was putting up a stiff resistance. The hole in his neck was widening and deepening and oozing what we now described as 'guts', the sort of bloody stuff we saw lying on the scullery table when our mother had eviscerated a herring. You could drop a two shilling piece into the crater.

My father was now in torturous pain. After his neck was bandaged he would pace the kitchen floor, cigarette between his fingers, his head stuck forward on his shoulders like a gun dog sniffing out a wounded duck in a marsh. Nobody complained. The odour of Kaolin dissipated under the smell of cigarette smoke. Somehow, there was always a packet of Woodbines or Players handy. But though the tension in the kitchen eased, our mother looked worried, and we sensed a threat in the air.

One evening, after she had removed the dressing and had inspected the boil, she reached the end of her tether: 'This boil's gettin' on my nerves, Billy. You'll have t' go t' th' hospital.'

He didn't argue. He knew you couldn't take chances with a voracious boil.

'I'll go with ye,' she added.

'No, no, it's aright, Mabel. I'll go m'self.'

'It's a long way t' th' Mater.'

'It's aright, nigh. I'll go m'self.'

They were on the edge of a barney, a quarrel. We watched, unsure whose side to take. Mother went to the hall and took her coat off a peg, and at that my father didn't say another word. She helped him put his coat on, and then turned to us:

'We won't be long nigh. Your Daddy'll be all right. So, youse behave yourselves.'

They left for the Mater Hospital, my mother quietly closing the door behind them.

Usually, when they went off to the pictures on a Friday night, leaving us to ourselves under my care, we could barely wait for their footsteps to disappear down the street, for we had the run of the house for two hours or so. The kitchen chairs would become a bomber aircraft or a tram, the kitchen, a hospital or even a church. The drawers in the rooms upstairs would be plundered, as out of curiosity we looked for God knows what.

But not this time. We had no enthusiasm for dropping bombs on Germans, collecting passengers or bandaging arms in splints taken from our father's St John Ambulance bag, or singing psalms and saying the Lord's Prayer at the pretend church services I conducted. We resisted the temptation to plunder; on a night like this, it didn't seem right. Instead, we tried to reassure each other that all father had was a big boil and the poultices would stop blood poisoning.

We sat at the fire grate, drowsily registered street sounds amplified in the night air: the rhythmic click-clack of high heels; the measured slap of brogues and clump of work boots, fading in and out beyond our front garden. Like cubs in a den, we stirred when we heard what we thought were familiar footfalls, and then settled again. On the mantelpiece our old clock every so often noisily gathered its strength, and chimed the quarter hours. Several came, and went.

Towards ten o'clock, the garden gate creaked, and two pairs of footsteps approached the front door.

As she took off her coat in the hall, mother announced before we could ask any questions, that father had a carbuncle. We broke into a litany of questions. What's a carbuncle? A boil, but bigger and sorer. Can it kill you? It can, but your father's is not so dangerous. What did they do at the hospital? The doctor examined it and the nurse cleaned it out. Does Daddy have to have more poultices? Yes, but we've ointment to put on his neck as well. Will the carbuncle get worse?

There was no answer to this question. Unless the clock on the mantelpiece held it, as it did the key to its own life.

In the days that followed, as each evening after tea time our father patiently submitted his neck to our mother's care, we asked: 'Is the carbuncle worse, Mammy?' We looked anxiously for an answer on her face as she unwrapped the bandage and removed the dry poultice. We looked for changes in the size of the hole, and were reassured when it had not become deeper nor wider.

Our questions became redundant before they had become tiresome, for soon the carbuncle ceased to ooze pus and the angry flesh slowly turned pink and the crater began to close. Our father's torment was over. But the carbuncle left its mark. Throughout the rest of his life, he bore in the nape of his neck a circular hollow scar, into which you could set a half-a-crown, the price of a couple of packets of cigarettes. Or a medal.

Epilogue

Our father's battle with the carbuncle became a touchstone by which in our family we measured our minor afflictions, such as a septic finger, a whitlow thumb, a sore toe. Remembering his endurance, we felt somewhat ashamed when we girned about our pains. But it was also a touchstone in another way.

At the reception after his funeral many years later – he died a year after he had retired from work – I found myself in conversation with some of his friends about his years in the shipyard, and we noted that except for the weeks he had pleurisy, he rarely missed a day's work. Then I remembered his carbuncle, and I saw him again, coming home from work, coming up the street at a steady pace, the white bandage around his neck, head bent forward. And it occurred to me, that in the course of a day he walked a lot, to and from the shipyard and as part of his job. The pain in his neck must have been killing him at times, and he must have had days when he questioned whether he should go to work. If so, his answer was always the same. He went.

Chapter 12

THE FORGER

MOST BIRTHDAYS merely nudge us into another year, but some dunt us in a significant direction, like an airplane thrust on a new course by a vertical wind; for example, in my case, toward school at the age of six to learn about the world, and, at the age of fourteen, into the shipyard to earn my way in that world. The birthdays between marked nothing more than an increasingly wider ring of candles on a cake to blow out, and another futile wish to make. My tenth was an exception. The dunt knocked me into a tail spin, and at the end of the day, I went to bed sorely bruised in my soul.

The day, a Wednesday, hadn't begun badly. On the contrary, I awoke in high hope, in the assurance that my life was about to take a flying leap forward into 'the realms of gold', and I swung out of bed with alacrity and without my mother having to shout my name up the stairs more than once. The cause of my uncharacteristic sudden wakefulness was not that I had now lived a decade – hardly a reason, in my view, for breaking one's habit of waking slowly – but that today I was going to join the library. And I would come home with a book under my arm to read after dinner.

For a long time I had been reading whatever I could get my hands on. At first, it was comic books, the *Hotspur*, *Wizard*, *Champion* and *Magnet*. They were not comic strips but more like magazines, the print not much larger than the tiny print in my Bible, and the story ran in columns, like the newspaper. You had to know how to read, and read well, to enjoy them. The only pictures in the comics were the drawings on the cover and at the head of each story. Since it was war time, the quality of the paper was poor.

My father disapproved of them for that reason. He believed that poor quality print was bound to harm my eyesight. As it was, my eyesight was as comparable to an eagle's as a human being's could be, and by the time

I moved on to Penguin paperbacks, it had not diminished one whit in sharpness. But this fact did not allay his fears; he considered paperback books to be harmful for the same reason that comics were. However, I treated his disapproval as merely a dissenting opinion, and ignored it. Each week with my pocket money I bought one of two comics; they were cheap, a few pennies each.

I couldn't go to sleep without a read. The bedroom, in which my brother, two sisters and I slept on a large bed, had only a ceiling light. Since they, being younger than I, went to bed to sleep, the light was put out after we had sorted ourselves out across the bed. The bedroom door was always left ajar. A shaft of light from the naked bulb hanging above the staircase landing wedged itself into the bedroom, a kind of night-light should any of us need to go to the bathroom. Often, within minutes of settling under the blankets, and the overcoats added for extra warmth during the damp cold winter months, one of us, to the annoyance of the others, would have to crawl urgently over everyone else. Being the eldest child, I slept on the outside of the bed and I could get out of and into bed a dozen times each night, without awakening anyone. But this arrangement had a more useful purpose, as far as I was concerned.

After mother had seen us to bed, she went back downstairs. I would listen for the sound of the kitchen door closing, and when it did, I would slip out of bed and open the bedroom door until the shaft of light from the landing partially struck my side of the bed. By twisting my torso, I could read a comic. Sometimes this posture caused a cramp in my side, but I would persevere. I had tried using my torch under a tent of blanket and coats, but with my siblings thrashing in their sleep I could scarcely get through a paragraph without the top of the tent sagging and the comic crumpling over like a shot gangster.

My only problem with reading by landing light was the uncertainty of time available for it. Mother would switch the light off, without warning, and sometimes at a suspenseful moment in a story I was reading, or even halfway through an unfamiliar word I was trying to sort out. Sometimes, she forgot about the light, and I read until my brain shut down or my eyelids collapsed, the comic dropping to the floor to be found by my mother on her way to bed. She was always warning me that my habit of reading in half-light would 'poke my eyes out'. That bothered me sometimes, and after a long spell of secret reading I would touch my eyeballs to see if they had moved out significantly from their sockets. To discourage me, for a night or two she would put out the light immediately we got into bed. This deterrent did not endear me to my siblings, but I couldn't expect them to understand; they weren't incorrigible readers.

Comic books satisfied me up to a point. I read them too quickly, my mother said, because no sooner had I finished one than I was begging for another. We had no books on shelves at home, no library at school. I had school readers which I read and reread. Then I discovered a bookcase of books. I had seen it week after week, year after year, and had paid no attention to it until one happy evening.

Every Sunday evening, Granda Morrison presided over a gathering of uncles, aunts, and our family, at his house on Oakley Street in the Ligoniel. The uncles and Daddy argued the toss about football, cricket, and occasionally politics, and filled the kitchen full of opinions and the air with cigarette smoke, except one uncle, who didn't smoke because he was religious, but nevertheless added his opinions. Granda didn't say much, smoked his pipe, spat into the fire, and now and again butted into the argument with an oath or two, which would cause Grandma to chastise him with tut-tuts and twiddles of her thumbs, 'Tommy, there's childer here.' If he heard her at all, he soon forgot. She was a short stout woman, whose family hailed from the Porters of Limavady, and who looked old to me, but never seemed to get any older as the years passed, and had borne ten children, two of whom had died in infancy.

While these arguments were in swing, my aunts would be in the scullery making tomato, lettuce, and egg sandwiches which we ate later with lashings of tea, which belied their invitation to 'a wee cup in yur hand before ye go'. My mother always forewarned us on our way to Grandma and Granda's that we were not to eat too many sandwiches, not to eat too quickly, and not to ask for more, lest Grandma should think our mother wasn't feeding us well enough.

We children usually sat on the lower stairs which connected the kitchen with the upstairs bedrooms, not speaking unless spoken to, finding something to laugh about when all the arguers argued at once, but often bored and, mindful of our mother's watchful but equally bored blue eyes, putting up with the boredom and with the irritating blue cigarette smoke without whimpering.

One evening, rather than finding a space on the stairs which ran down one wall of the kitchen, I took a book out of the small bookcase behind Granda's chair near the fireplace, and sat down behind his chair to read it. It was not like the comics, and I expected it to bore me, but it didn't.

Squatting on the floor beside the bookcase, week by week, I read until Daddy called out it was time to 'make tracks', to go home. The titles alone opened my imagination wider than the stories in comics: *Coral Island*, *Tom Brown's Schooldays*, *Travels* (of Mungo Park) *in the Interior Districts of Africa in the years 1795, 1796, and 1797, Treasure Island, Midshipman Easy, Two Years before the Mast*. Had my grandfather read them? My uncles? My father? I didn't ask, but when I mentioned the titles to my father, he seemed to recognise them. But nothing more was said. I wasn't allowed to take any of the books with me, and so, I had to remember where I left off, which meant remembering all that had gone before.

It was my mother who said to my father, one Sunday evening as we walked home from Oakley Street, a twenty- to thirty-minute walk, depending on your 'bend', your pace and length of stride:

'He's ready for th' liberty, so he is.'

'Can I join tamarra?' I asked her.

'Ye cin join when you're ten,' she said. 'That's only a month or two away. Ye cin wait that long.'

I could, and I couldn't. I had the taste of good words on my tongue, and my stomach was rumbling.

My tenth birthday took its time arriving: the days dandered along as if they were on a Sunday walk. When it did, I arose before my brother and sisters, a rare event, and raised the window blind to see if the sun had arrived too. It had. It was a fine May morning.

The hours at school crawled more slowly than usual, and when they reached their end, I raced home, dumped my old schoolbag behind the front door, and shouted to my mother where I was going. I had no time to lose. She cautioned me to be careful crossing the streets, to watch out for trams, and suggested that I drop in on Granda Porter on the way home. I tore down the street like a mitching schoolboy fleeing a school inspector.

The North Belfast Branch Library, on the Oldpark Road, was quite a distance away, near the junction of Crumlin Road and Agnes Street. If you stayed on the tram for downtown, you would pass the Belfast Courthouse and the Crumlin Jail. A huge statue of a blindfolded woman holding in one hand the scales of justice and in the other, a sword, stood on the courthouse roof, dominating the skyline. Across the road, and behind a high iron railing, lay the prison, a large three- or four-storied stone building with a huge iron door and long rows of cell windows. You would see, often, arms waving from the small barred windows, and you would want to wave back. Sometimes, as I passed it on the tram I did, and then felt stupid for surely whoever had waved couldn't see me.

Had I the halfpenny for the fare, I could have taken a tram to the library but I had just enough money for my library ticket, and that I had sunk securely in the depth of my trouser pocket. Instead, I ran, and when a stitch threatened my side, I walked it out and ran again: up Deerpark Road, along the Oldpark Road past the Park Picture House, past Finiston School where Mammy had tried to enroll me when I was six but the school had no room for me, past the Sacred Heart Church in the Catholic Bone, but on the other side, in case I was accosted by Fenians and be delayed, past the street where my Granda lived and the pub where he got drunk sometimes, past the bread shop where he bought his crumpets for his wee cups of tea, past the butcher's shop with its row of skinned rabbits hanging outside its window and, at the bend of the road, past the flower and vegetable shop where my mother worked before she got married.

At the bend, the library came into view, and I increased my pace for the final sprint past a row of houses with parlour windows, until out of breath, my jersey sticking to my back, my trousers to my bum, and my socks around my ankles, I stumbled up steps into the library hallway.

The library door swung open and a woman came out, and before the door swung shut I caught a glimpse of high book-lined shelves. As she came down the steps of the vestibule, I glanced up at her, and then at the books under her arm. Three. A real reader, she is. I stepped up to the door and slowly pushed it until it emptied me, suddenly, into the library.

A heavy odour of floor polish and varnish rushed to my head, like the smell of ammonia my mother used for cleaning windows. I couldn't breathe for a minute. The place felt like a church, and as quiet as a long night. Instead of pews, long rows of bookcases filled with books stretched from wall to wall, except where there were desks like long tables, at which a few old men and some children older than me sat bent over books. The library windows were high and narrow with small square panes of glass. The dark varnished bookshelves and tables shone in the light from the windows and from the globes hanging from the ceiling. A cough perforated the stillness, and then silence returned, as if someone had pinched with their fingers a rent in a curtain that had leaked out light.

My brain spun. How will I choose from so many books? How many will I be allowed to take home, and for how long? I didn't know; none of my friends went to the library.

To my right there was a low counter behind which a bespectacled man sat at a large desk reading a book. He seemed to be an old man, near my Granda Morrison's age, I supposed, and like Granda, was bald. I tapped a little bell on the counter to attract his attention, not a hard tap, a tentative one because I didn't want to disturb him if he was too busy. I didn't want to get off on the wrong foot; joining the library was a very serious business. He looked up, and stood, and I saw at once that he was a very important man, with a gold chain across the front of his waistcoat.

'Sir,' I said, 'I'm here t' join the liberty.'
He leaned over the counter until his face seemed to hover over me, and examined me through his spectacles as if he had me under a microscope.

'You want to join the library?'
He pronounced 'library' slowly, with emphasis, as if I hadn't said the word properly.

'Yis, sir.'

'How old are you?'

'Ten, sir. I was ten yisterday.'

'You don't look ten-years-old.'

'But I am. My Mammy cudn't come wi' me and vouch for me age, an' she said it would be all right if I came on me own an' tole the man at the liberty what age I wis.'

I began to feel nervous. His voice sounded like a schoolmaster's, full of authority, not the sort of voice you'd want to argue with. My face heated up as if I had been running again. He reached beneath the counter and pulled out a long piece of paper. That was a good sign; he wasn't turfing me out. I stood on tiptoes to gain an extra inch and show my interest in the paper.

'This is an application form for children who wish to join the library. You can fill it in yourself, your name and address and date of birth here and here.'

He pointed with his fountain pen at spaces on the paper, and I relaxed. It's happening, I'm now joining the library. Then he moved his pen toward the bottom of the page.

'You have to have your mother or father sign here as your guarantor,' he said.

'Garnter?'

He sensed rightly that I didn't know what he was talking about. The hallway seemed to darken.

''G-u-a-r-a-n-t-o-r'. Someone has to promise that you will return your books, and pay for any books you might damage or lose.'

He spoke slowly and loudly, as a schoolmaster does when he thinks you're stupid. I wanted to shout, 'I'm nat deef nor an edjit,' but I held my tongue. This was no time to fight with him. I felt a sudden fear that I would not leave the library with a book. Then I had an inspiration:

'Cud my Granda sign th' form?'

'Where does your Granda live?'

'Just up the road. Ballymena Street.'

'Yes. Your grandfather can sign in place of your father and mother, so long as he adds his address.'

The world brightened again, as if the sun had shouldered a cloud aside to throw some light on this matter. On the large round clock on the wall above the man's desk two spidery hands were pointing at Roman numerals X and IV.

'Thanks, sir. What time does the liberty close?'

'*Library*. This is Wednesday, and the library is not open on Wednesday evenings. We close at five o'clock.'

'I'll git me Granda t' sign it an' be back.'

I was disappointed, but things could have been worse. I was pleased with my quick thinking. If I had to go home to get the form signed, I wouldn't have got back to the library before it closed. Granda Porter lived five minutes running time from here, and if I ran both ways, I would be back in time to get my ticket and have enough time left for a quick look in the children's section and take out a book. Maybe two, but I didn't want to be seen as greedy on my first day.

Granda Porter was sitting on the table beside the window, sewing the bottom leg of a pair of long trousers. He was a retired shipyard worker, and had a knack for tailoring. For a wee fee he mended and adjusted coats and trousers for neighbours. I liked to visit with him, have a wee chat about this and that. He always made me a cup of tea, but this time, I explained to him, I didn't have time for tea, and needed him to sign a library form for me. I showed him the line where he had to sign. It was such a straightforward matter that I was surprised when he said,

'You just put my name there.'

'But YOU have t' write it, Granda.'

'Me eyes are nat so good an' these glasses nat the best.'

'Dye think that'll be aright? Won't they know I'd wrote it?'

'Be aright, son. Them libery people don't bather much about things like that.'

I wasn't so sure. The man at the library didn't seem to be the sort of person who wouldn't bother. I rummaged in the sideboard drawer, found a pen and a bottle of ink, and took it to Granda with the hope that if I put a pen in his hand he would sign. He didn't put down the trousers he was sewing:

his hand moved expertly and rhythmically along the seam at the bottom of one leg. I shifted about from one foot to another. Granda turned from one trouser leg to the other. The clock on his mantelpiece ticked away precious time.

Unable to stand the tension any longer I sat down at one end of the table where I had room to fill in the form. A ripple of pleasure ran through me as I wrote down my birth date and age. When I came to the bottom of the page, where the word GUARANTOR stood out in bold black letters, I could hear the voice pronouncing the word, with emphasis, as if he was underlining it with a black marker, and a pinprick of anxiety punctured my mood.

I read out word by word the guarantor's declaration for my Granda's benefit, hitting each word distinctly as if they were nails I was pounding into the yard door. When I finished reading I looked up, but my Granda was still bent over the trouser cuff, his needle, ever so fine between his fingers that you could hardly see it, rising on the end of a thread and plunging back again into the cloth like a fisherman raising and casting his hook into a trout stream. He showed no sign of having heard me. I dipped the pen in the bottle of ink again, shook off the surplus, and readied myself for the feat ahead.

'I know yur name's James Porter but what's all of yur name, Granda?'

'James S. Porter.'

'What's the 'S' stand fer?'

''Samuel'. But ye don't need t' write it down, just th' initial 'll do.'

Slowly and with deliberation I wrote *James S. Porter*. The letters looked larger than my Granda might write, and I had smudged the top curve of the 'S' because I hadn't shaken off excess ink carefully enough. I looked for blotter in the sideboard drawer but found none, and so I waved the form to make the ink dry more quickly. The small blob inside the top of the 'S' ran a little.

I showed Granda the signature, and he nodded his approval. The mantelpiece clock whirred and banged out the half hour past four o'clock to tell me to get a bend on if I was to return to the library before it closed. Taking leave of Granda with a promise to be back soon, I hit the street at a run. As I pounded my way along the footpath back to the library, I worried about the wee blot in the 'S'. The man at the library might catch on that I had signed the form. I should explain to him why I did so before he asks, and maybe it will be all right.

On the library steps I leaned against a wall to catch my breath – I didn't want to be speechless nor to look bothered at this critical moment. A minute later, my wits now about me, I presented myself at the counter. The man took the form and perused it. His glasses tipped toward the bottom of the page, and I gripped the edge of the counter to steady myself before I spoke, but before I could begin to explain my predicament, he asked,

'Your grandfather signed this?'

He leaned toward me, so closely that I could see clearly a few strands of hair stuck across his bald head like fine dark wires.

'Tell him, tell him now,' a voice in my head insisted. I paused, and the pause gave me time to gather enough courage to lie.

'Yis, sir.'

'And his name is James S. Porter?'

The voice in my head urged, 'Not too late to tell him the truth'.

'Yis, sir.'

'This is not your grandfather's signature, is it?'

Obviously, the mess around the 'S' had given me away. I made a weak effort to convince him.

'Ye see, sir, his eyes is nat so good an' the nib spilt.'

But even as I said this I realised that of all things that was the biggest lie. His eyes were good enough to thread the needle you could hardly see held between his fingers, and good enough to stitch the black cuff of black trousers so neatly you could not see the thread, and good enough to sign my flipping library application form. My anger shifted from the bald head to my Granda. The bald head spoke:

'You're telling me a lie. I can see from how you write your own name that you signed your grandfather's name.'

How could he see that, I wondered? Should I argue with him, maintain that my Granda signed the form, and hope to persuade him? Too much was at stake. I needed the library like a drunk needed a pub. He continued, and his voice sounded now like a policeman who has caught you red-handed:

'That's forgery, you know, and forgery is a crime.'

My knees trembled, and I felt a sudden need to pee. Was he going to call a peeler to come and lift me, a forger, like the fellows in the sunshades and shirtsleeves printing fake pound notes under a hanging light bulb in a grubby room? I'd be taken to the Courthouse, maybe the jail: no, I'm a boy, I would be sent to the Balmoral Boys' Home at the top of our street, or worse, to a Borstal. *But it's only my Granda's name!* I wanted to shout at him. My wits left me, like marbles spilling through a hole in my trouser pocket and rolling off in all directions.

I stammered the truth, and as I did so I realised two things almost simultaneously: first, he wouldn't know for sure if it was the truth and that I had not just whipped around the corner to the nearest entry and filled in the form, complete with the forged signature, and second, and much worse, that I was not going to be able to take any books out of the library before it closed, and maybe not ever. I might be barred. Forgers can't be trusted, ever. At this thought, I was on the verge of tears, but held them in check. To make a spectacle of myself by blubbering on top of being caught lying was too much humiliation to bear.

Despite the serious position I was in, and as far as I could see, I hoped that the truth might soften him enough to drop the forgery charge, for a start. When it seemed that he wasn't going to call for a policeman, I had another hope, a faint one. Maybe he would let me have a library ticket now if I promised to bring a properly-signed form back tomorrow, even though what I had done didn't say much in my favour.

'Cud I git me ticket nigh an' bring my Mammy's signature tamarra?'

'Here's a new form. You have your Mammy sign it and bring it back, and you'll get your library ticket tomorrow. We'll say no more about it.'

'Yis, sir.'

His voice had lost its severity, but I could see that there was no use begging him, because that is what any arguing on my part would have amounted to. The watery clock on the wall indicated that the library would be closing in ten minutes. I took the form, and left.

On the steps of the library I could no longer restrain myself and I wept, and my nose joined in from sympathy and soon the sleeve of my jersey was a mess. A tram thundered and shrieked past on its way down to join the Crumlin Road.

At least, I hadn't been barred, I told myself. But what I had done, innocently enough, troubled me. Why was I so stupid to think that a signature forged by a boy could convince a grown-up? And what impulse made me lie when I knew a lie was not only wrong but futile? And why didn't I argue with Granda that there was nothing wrong with his eyesight? He read the newspaper, didn't he, while he sat opposite me beside the range in his kitchen, the two of us drinking tea, his in a small bowl and mine in a cup? I had been stupid, and paid for my stupidity. And that truth was in my soul like a tiny stone inside my shoe on the long slow walk home. But I was not without consolation.

On my way, I paused for a rest at the top of the hill where the Church of St Silas stood before it was fire bombed by the Germans. From there you can see lying below you the streets of our district and beyond them the hillside sloping upward towards Divis Mountain, and the smoke from hundreds of chimney pots rising and leaning into the air and dissolving into the sky above. Dry-eyed now, I put my left hand into my pocket and felt a three penny bit, the money for my library ticket. I had forgotten it because I hadn't needed it. It was warm with the heat of my body. I grasped it, tightly, for I would be needing it tomorrow.

My mother heard my story with sympathy, blamed my grandfather, cursed the librarian for his officiousness, and signed as my guarantor. The two layer birthday cake she had baked with cream in the middle and coloured icing on top assuaged my grief as a mild analgesic temporarily relieves a toothache, and I blew out the candles solely to confirm the strength of my lungs, nothing more.

On the following day, I returned to the library, handed the form to the librarian, who greeted me, 'You're back', scanned the form, made no reference to my criminal offence, and took a brand new library ticket out of a drawer. He wrote in it, and handed it to me. The ticket was two narrow pieces of thick cardboard about two and a half inches long which were covered with black cloth and hinged, so that, opened, it showed, in the librarian's neat handwriting, my name and borrower's number. I gave him the three penny bit and he handed me the ticket. Did he smile? Perhaps. I would like to think so. I did, but maybe not at him. I scanned my name on the ticket, with its middle initial, 'P', for 'Porter'. For a brief moment thought that I should apologise for yesterday's debacle, but I didn't want to open a wound which had begun to heal, and said only 'Thanks, sir,' and slid the ticket into the left pocket of my trousers.

The hour I spent cruising the shelves in the children's section of the library was among the happiest in my childhood. I had only myself to please and nobody to tell me what to choose. It was hard to decide which among the titles on the spines I should borrow. I saw *Coral Island*, and felt pleased with myself that I had already read it. *Peter The Whaler* took my fancy because it too was about sailing ships. I presented the book and my ticket to the librarian. Without a word he stamped the strip of paper inside its front cover with the return date, two weeks hence. I could see from the list of dates above mine that many other readers had made the same choice. Satisfied, I tucked the book securely under my arm. I put my ticket securely in my pocket, and thrust the library door open.

And on the library steps, I was lifted by a wind and carried away.

Chapter 13

GRAFFITI

DOOT McCULLOUGH and Mr Taylor taught Fifth Standard at Everton Elementary School, and you were unlucky one way or another when you passed into their classes after the long wanton weeks of summer. Or lucky, according to your point of view. Both views were aired in the 'bog' on the last morning of school before the holidays. The 'bog', or boys' lavatory, sat at the perimeter of the school playground. It held a row of cubicles sheltered under a narrow roof, and a urinal, a long high brick wall, exposed to the unholy elements. The wall bore an assortment of crude etchings made with rusty nails, blunt penknives and sharp stones: initials, dates, disclosures of who loves whom, misshapen hearts, and obscenities about Hitler, the Pope, and certain masters.

We had been 'let out' for our usual midmorning pee – in our world a 'recess' was a nook in the kitchen where the wireless sat – and stood in a line facing the wall, fiddling with the buttons on the front of our trousers.

'Who' ye gitin' fer Fifth Stannar?'

'Doot.'

'Yer lucky. He's aisy.'

'But ye'll learn nathin' in his class, an' that makes it hard fer ye when ye go inta Copey's for Sixth. So evirybody says.'

'Who' ye gitin'?'

'Taylor.'

'Yer in fer't. He shouts an' slaps ye fer nathin'. He split somedee's han' open wi'his cane an' his morr came up to th' school an' there was a barging match, but didn't stap Taylor usin' his cane. Somedee's big brawer or uncle shud hammer him, but nobody does.'

'But he makes ye learn.'

Nobody challenged this claim. Piss crackled like small whips against the wall and water gurgled along the scupper. I kept my thoughts to myself. The prospect of getting up in the morning to face Taylor day in and day out for almost a year sent a twinge through my kidneys.

It was easy to hate Taylor but it wasn't easy to learn under him, as far as I was concerned. Earlier in the year, for a reason now annihilated by time, I had spent a week in his class. Taylor was the youngest master in the school, a big black-haired fellow with large blue eyes that bulged from their sockets when he was mad. Each morning after roll-call he took a thick willow cane out of his cupboard and flicked it to make sure it hadn't by some boy's magic softened like a stick of liquorice during the night. The cane had frayed at the tip with use and it cut through the air with a whistle like Basil Rathbone's sword in *The Sea Hawk*.

Taylor bellowed so much as he walked the aisles between the desks while you did your sums, that the numbers you were feverishly muttering to yourself as you added column after column were frightened into oblivion, and so you either took too long to finish the sum, or got it wrong. In either case, you thought yourself fortunate if he barged you or whacked the back of your head with his hand. If he was in a foul mood he might raise a welt or two the size of penny baps on the palm of your hand with his cane.

The scupper trickled into silence. Relieved and buttoned up, we filed out of the bog and scattered into the sunlit playground. Somebody dropped and kicked a bald tennis ball across the concrete playground, and as everyone tore after it into the six carefree weeks of summer, I shouted above the fracas:

'But after a year wi' Taylor, yir back id be as straight as an Irish Guard's.' There was a brief cackle, but I was serious. There was that to be said for Taylor.

For fifteen minutes at the beginning of class each morning, he made you sit upright, shoulders back, arms hooked over the backrest of your desk. If he saw you slouch, he ordered you to get the floor brush from the cupboard where he kept his cane, hold it horizontally behind your shoulder blades in the crook of your arms, and stand at the back of the room, sort of crucified on the brush, until he noticed you again. Maybe in half-an-hour. He told us that we should do this exercise, as he called this sort of torture, at home. It would keep our backs straight as we grew up. I believed him. I wanted my back to be straight, but not because I wanted to be an Irish Guard. The Guards regiments didn't take recruits under six feet tall, and I knew that at my rate of growth, I wouldn't have been able to add enough cubits to my stature, to borrow the words of Jesus, to be eligible for their ranks, no matter how often I touched my toes without bending. Not even if I never smoked one cigarette. But, at least, by trying I could have a short straight stature.

My brother and sisters coming upon me draped on the floor brush thought I was acting the fool, as usual. My mother wondered aloud if I had the head staggers, and ordered me into the backyard because I might knock the clock off the mantelpiece. But at least I saved her having to waste her breath telling me not to slouch at the dining table. My father cautioned, 'That'll keep yir back straight, son, but mind ye don't poke anybody's eye out.'

Within a week my enthusiasm for a back as straight as a new poker petered out, and I consoled myself for my dereliction of duty to King and country with the comforting belief that in the Royal Navy, bandy legs for standing on the tossing decks of ships were more useful than a straight back, and easy to acquire if you walk hen-toed all the time. Still, for a while afterwards, if I suspected that I was getting a hump, I would reach for the floor brush and take it into the backyard.

II

Mr McCullough, to give him his respectful name, was a descendant of a duke. So he had said in an unguarded moment. For a time he was 'Duke' McCullough until a wit, mimicking one of the Dead End Kids, dubbed him 'Doot'. He was, moreover, 'very devout'. He was a member of the Plymouth Brethren, a Christian sect whose adherents didn't smoke, drink, dance, go to the pictures, or, in some cases, listen to the wireless, and who went to a Gospel Hall rather than a church or chapel. He was reputed to preach often while he taught.

Doot's classroom looked much the same as the others I had been in since Senior Infants. The master's desk, close by a window, was cluttered with books and papers, a box of chalk, a small pair of scales, a pile of thin squares of various metals, and a Bible. Like Taylor, he had a cane, but, he said on our first day of class, he preferred to keep it in his cupboard. For the benefit of those of us who were too thick to understand the significance of this information, he explained that he trusted us to behave ourselves. His voice was not loud, like Taylor's, and its tone was friendly, avuncular. Before I passed into his class I had paid no attention to him, but now, sitting in a desk in the fourth row from the front I took a good look at him in his navy suit with a fine stripe, and waistcoat of the same cloth, and spectacles with heavy black rims. His eyes behind the glasses were dark. Thinking of how devout he was, I wondered what he did for fun and then realised that I also wondered what any teacher did for fun, and so the question was redundant.

True to his reputation, Doot strayed from time to time into the fields of the Lord, usually in the afternoon, and we pastured there for the rest of the day. In those early weeks most of us didn't mind that we were hearing more about God and Jesus than geometry and history, because we weren't having to do much of what we were supposed to do in school. It was not the case that Doot didn't teach us anything. We had lessons on history, geography, algebra, lessons on weights and measurements. We did sums in our jotters, read stories from our readers, exercised our grammar, and wrote compositions. No revolt of the masses hungry for an education or baying for a tyrant's blood brewed in the bog, for we had the measure of Doot and cannily had learned how to open the gate into idle afternoons. 'Doot was all right,' we said. And some of us basked in his grace.

I was content. I had no dreams of scholastic glory, and the religion Doot talked in class was much the same as I was hearing elsewhere, at the Presbyterian Sunday school to which I was sent, with my brother and sisters every Sunday afternoon, while our parents had their Sunday nap. On Friday nights, mainly for something to do, I went with some friends to a 'wee meetin' for boys in a Mission Hall at the bottom of our street, where we sang choruses, prayed, heard Bible stories, and frequently got 'saved' by Jesus from the penalty of our sins.

One day Doot handed out small rectangles of blotting paper which advertised a meeting at Oldpark Gospel Hall, next door to the Park Cinema, where often you would find me on the Saturday afternoons I wasn't at the matinee in the Forum Cinema in Ardoyne. The free blotting paper was welcome, of course, since we had to buy our own, and often made do with an old bit that was so covered with ink blots and bits of backward words you needed a magnifying glass to find a clear spot. The real attraction of the meeting was the bag of sweets you earned if you recited 'word perfect' texts from the Bible. With sweets being rationed by the government to two ounces each week, the offer was hard to resist.

So, between attending 'wee meetings', where with a hall full of sweet-starved hopefuls, I belted out the chorus, 'Tangles, tangles, tangles I was in / I was born in Tangle Town because of Adam's sin', and attending Sunday school – where I was learning by heart psalms, hymns, chunks of the Bible and the Shorter Catechism (all one hundred and seven questions and answers which I didn't understand but was told I would by and by) – I was as literate as an eleven-year-old boy could be in the King James Bible, and in the vocabulary of sin and salvation, grace and damnation.

Sometimes, in bed beside my sleeping brother and sisters, with the light out and my fancy switched on, I would think of Hell and break into a kind of religious night-sweat. My sins would rise up before me and sit on the side of the bed, arms folded and looking glum: going to the pictures, fibbing, cursing, stealing apples from the crate outside the greengrocer's at Cliftonville Circus, spitting at cats, bad thoughts, and for good measure, hitting my brother and sisters even if I couldn't remember actually having done so. I would have a fleeting moment of relief that I was too young to have sinned by smoking, drinking stout and dancing in dens of iniquity, like the Plaza and the Floral Hall Ballrooms. In a single swift short mutter, I would confess my sins, ask Jesus into my heart and hope that God wouldn't mind me getting saved while I was in bed rather than kneeling on the cold oilcloth. My sins would vanish, and I would fall asleep. This state of grace would last until the next Saturday matinee at the Forum or the Park, when again I would put my soul in jeopardy for the sake of the pleasures of the world. Backsliding. That's what Doot would say I was doing.

One afternoon he picked up the class roll, opened it, traced his finger down each page as if scanning for absentees, looked straight at us and asked,

'Boys and girls, are your names in the Book of Life?'

We stopped what we were doing, if we were doing anything at all. He told us that whoever's name was not in the book would be cast into the lake of fire, and quoted from the Book of Revelation to support this news, as if any of us were likely to contradict him. You didn't argue with Doot, nor with God. God was God, and Doot was our schoolmaster who knew more about God than we did.

It is one thing to be warned about Hell while you were waiting to see if you would earn a bag of sweets, but another when your own master warns you about it. I had always thought of it as a place like the quarries near Cave Hill but where the rocks were red hot and sparks of brimstone swirled in the smoky air like the shower of a roman candle on a foggy November night. The lake of fire was new to me, and not hard to imagine if you had seen, as I had from the hill at the top of our street, the blazing sky over Belfast on the night German bombers in their hundreds fire-bombed the city.

While Doot told us how we could get our names into the Book of Life, my mind lingered on that lake. I had seen in a book a picture of souls tumbling in yellow sulphurous air and vanishing head first into a cauldron of fire. Angels, their wings unsinged, were tossing white wriggling souls into a fiery pit as if they were chucking them into Peter's Hill Swimming Baths, or into the Glenbank Mill dam, which I never passed without a shudder, because each summer one or two boys, tangled in its weeds, drowned there. I couldn't swim, but that didn't matter as far as the lake of fire was concerned.

I took my infernal thoughts home to mull over them. The punishment for not being enrolled in the Book of Life, and for going to the pictures, seemed excessive, but I wasn't about to argue with Doot about it. Besides, the lake of fire wasn't the sort of thing you asked questions about, except to find out how to stay out of it. It was geography, yet it didn't fit with learning about Lough Neagh, the biggest lake in Ireland. But you could ask Doot anything about the Second Coming, and get an answer that would distract him for the rest of the afternoon.

Like most Plyms, he knew the Bible back to front and sideways, quite literally, because he could pick a text in Revelation and before you knew it you were in Exodus or Leviticus, running around the Tabernacle in the wilderness with the children of Israel or even back in the Garden of Eden. And he knew all about the end of the world. He could explain Ezekiel's visions and Daniel's dreams and sort out the timetable in the book of Revelation and tell you who Gog and Magog were, and who the Anti-Christ might be (though we already knew who he was). He knew the meaning of 666, carved on the foreheads of the unsaved like the mark of Zorro, and when the Great Tribulation would begin and where the awesome battle of Armageddon would be fought, a battle more fierce than the battle of the Somme, which we commemorated each July First, or El Alamein where Monty sent Rommel running back to Germany. It was more exciting than history because it was the future.

For Doot, the end of the world was always near, next weekend maybe, and you might come out of the pictures on a Saturday afternoon, your head splitting with a headache brought on by the sudden burst of daylight after two hours wallowing in the darkness of iniquity, and find the Second Coming in progress and nobody at home to make your tea. Worse, with the world ending you wouldn't have the thrill of leaving school, and of having money to go to the pictures at night and sit in the balcony seats and contentedly blow cigarette smoke into the darkness, or watch it curl into the widening cone of white light that sped downwards and burst into life on a screen far below. Sinning would be over and done with.

The trouble with Doot was that he got personal. One afternoon, we had settled down for a lesson on algebra. Doot had written some problems on the blackboard, and we were copying them into our jotters. When he sat down, Alex Harper asked him, 'Sir, how will we know the Second Coming is here?' I put my pencil down, and slung my arms over the back of the desk in the best Taylorian manner. Doot stood up, moved to the front of his desk, half-sat on it, and folded his arms. He began:

'Two men are working in a field. Suddenly, one vanishes. Two women are grinding flour for bread. In the blink of an eye...'

He snapped his fingers, and we blinked to measure the instant, and Doot went on, having captured our attention:

'...one is taken, the other left. The Second Coming is here, and all the saved on earth have gone up to meet their Lord in the air. For Jesus has come in clouds of glory, as He promised.'

My head swivelled to the classroom windows, beyond which clouds were drifting in the grey sky toward Divis Mountain. I half-expected to see crowds of people milling around, and among them a sweaty reaper stripped to the waist and scythe still in hand, like Victor Hale, to whose farm I had been evacuated after the Blitz, and a woman like Jinny, his wife, with her hair in a turban and her pinny covered in flour, and her clabbered water boots showing below the hem of her dress.

Then I remembered seeing the same sort of thing at the pictures, where, at the end of the picture, people who had died in the story appeared again among clouds, and though you were glad to seem them again, you knew it was trick photography, and felt a bit disappointed. Doot went on:

'It's called "The Rapture", boys and girls, "The Rapture".'

The word sounded like an injury you could do to yourself trying to lift a wet sandbag, or like the huge belly laugh that rolled around Cliftonville Football Ground, when the big centre-half booted the ball over the grandstand into the nearby street. But, thinking that way about the Rapture was as bad as swearing.

Doot now had forgotten entirely about the algebra on the blackboard. He described how happy that meeting in the air would be for the saved from all over the world, from China and India and Africa and America, and of course from Belfast. Even people from history would be there, because they would rise from their graves to join in.

A hand shot up, as if its arm had been sprung loose by a trigger:

'Sir, what'll happen to them that's not in the Rapture?'

His voice dropped, and his tone became sorrowful. I unhooked my arms from the back of my desk. Doot spoke quietly now:

'On those that are left great calamities will fall.'

He gave an example: a driverless tram careening down the hill of the Crumlin Road because the saved tram driver had been taken to meet his Lord. You could see it slam into the Forum Picture House just as the sinners were getting out. The class entered into the catastrophic spirit; we delved into our imaginations and called out for his approval all sorts of calamities: trains running off the rails and ships running on to rocks, runaway horses and carts, all because saved train drivers and ships' captains and coalmen had disappeared in the blink of an eye. It would be worse than the Blitz. Worse than an earthquake. And it would be happening all over the world. We were on the edge of becoming as noisily excited as a crowd at a western on a Saturday afternoon. Doot cut into our fantasies with a sobering warning:

'Jesus said, "Two men shall be sleeping in the same bed. One shall be taken, the other left. Saved parents will be taken up and their unsaved children will be left behind."'

He paused to let his words hit home. An air-locked radiator in the classroom knocked against the silence, and you could feel the heat of the calamities chill into this terrifying prospect. I hadn't thought of the Second Coming being like that. Stevie, who sat beside me, was an orphan and often wore old ragged trousers too big for him. Orphans, I believed, had miserable lives. Doot's eyes scanned our faces. It seemed as though he was looking at you and everybody else at the same time. He raised one hand and pointed a finger here, there, at random, as if he was about to call you to the front of the class.

'That boy beside you, that girl beside you, might be taken up, and you would be left.'

Somebody giggled, and the sombre mood for a moment teetered, and Doot frowned, and the mood steadied itself. I had a cheeky thought too, but kept it off my tongue, for I felt uneasy and unwilling to risk neither Doot's nor God's damnation. But I would miss Stevie if he went up in his arseless trousers to meet the Lord in the air, and left me behind.

The square of sky outside the window was silent and empty and grey but for a few clouds. The thought that at any moment they might split asunder, and a shining white figure would appear, like the picture I had seen on a religious card, and above his head, in wisps of cloud like a Spitfire's slipstream, would be written the words, 'Behold, He cometh', and, in that moment the whole sky would be crowded with souls and would split its sides with laughter, was awesome, terrifying, but wonderful. Doot made the Second Coming feel real.

You could hardly hear him now. In a quiet voice he told us to bow our heads and close our eyes. There was a shuffle as bodies shifted and heads dropped, some on to arms folded on the tops of desks, so that your nose sucked up the odour of stale varnish and ink, and God knows, fifty years of sweat from grubby palms, including your own. You couldn't see if everybody's eyes were closed, and you didn't want Doot to catch you peering left or right along your row of desks to see if everybody in them were doing as they were told. I shut my eyes tightly and held my breath. A minute later he told us to lift our heads.

He had turned back to the algebra he had left idling on the blackboard. There was an air of sheepishness in the classroom. Whispers could be heard here and there. 'Did you do it?' 'Naw.' 'Yer lyin'. 'Naw, I'm nat,' as if we had been into mischief. Nobody wanted to admit that Doot had given him the willies. There wasn't much left of the afternoon, and the algebra became our homework. I kept the faith for a while, until a Western starring my favourite cowboy, William Boyd (Hopalong Cassidy), came to the Park Cinema, and I risked missing the Rapture to enjoy a transient pleasure.

Sometime later, Doot went too far, I thought. He told us about his sad task after the Blitz of drawing lines through names in the class roll of a few girls and boys who had been killed. They were taken suddenly, he said, and he reminded us that we might not have time to repent of our sins. There was a stiff silence in the classroom. Each of us knew he or she might have been one of the scratched names. Doot was easy, if by that one means he rarely caned you for mistakes, but I had begun to dislike him. You would have had to be thick to miss his unspoken question hanging over that sad roll call.

Then I fell from his grace. The cause was a joke, literally, a joke.

III

Now and again, for a change of pace between lessons, Doot would ask if anyone in the class had a good joke to tell, and hands went up, and we would hear the inane jokes and riddles some of us had come upon in the *Beano* or *Dandy* comics or in *The Boy's Own Paper*. Since no other schoolmaster in the school offered such an invitation to us in the middle of our lessons, we liked Doot for it. One boy said he did it because he wanted us to like him, and others agreed. I did want to like him, but not for that reason, and so I was thrown into a quandary.

One late spring afternoon, as we were settling into class after lunch, Doot called for jokes. On impulse, I put up my hand. He hushed the class:

'Morrison? Well, go ahead, Morrison.'

My heart thumped. I took a deep breath, and the words stampeded out of my mouth like ants scattering from under an upturned peever:

'There's these boys, sir, who're bein' chased by a man because they'd broke a windy in his house wi' a wee ball they wure playin' futball wi' in th' street. Th' man knew only one av thim an' his name was Dunn. They hooked it...'

'Take your time, Morrison. You mean 'they ran away'?'

'Yes, sir, an' come to a public lavarty where they hid but th' man saw thim goin' in an' when he got till th' lavarty he went in to have a look, an' all th' doors where ye sit were shut. So th' man went along rapping on th' doors and shouting 'Are ye Dunn?' an' one voice says 'Naw, I'm Coulter' an' anorer says 'Naw, I'm McCormick' an' anorer says 'Naw, I'm Brown.''

Some boys, thinking I had come to the end of the joke, sniggered. I paused to gather breath for the last spurt to the end of the story:

'Dunn, who was sittin' on th' seat cud hear th' man comin', an' he was wonderin' what name he should shout out – but he didn't have time to make one up, for th' man rapped on th' door an' shouted 'Are ye Dunn?' an' Dunn shouted back, 'Naw, I've only started.''

The class erupted, and I sat down, pleased with myself. The laughter stopped as suddenly as it had started, and I looked at Doot. Behind his black-rimmed glasses his eyes had hardened into black marbles and transfixed me. Something was wrong, and I felt a chill, the kind I felt on the occasions he did use his cane, for he could be vicious.

'Where did you hear that joke, Morrison?'

'From my friends, sir.'

'Filthy, Morrison. I never want to hear anyone ever tell a filthy joke like that in my class.'

Everyone stared at Doot. He spoke with vehemence, as if he had been

offended, as if I had deliberately told the joke because it would offend him
The class sat still, as if gripped by a stiff silence. I made no attempt to
defend myself. Doot quoted Jesus, saying that it was not what goes into
the mouth defiles a man, but that which comes out of his mouth, and now
that Jesus had been brought into the matter, I felt ashamed, even though I
couldn't see how the joke was filthy.

I waited for him to take his cane from the cupboard. Instead, he warned
us against 'bad companions', about the broad way that led to destruction. He
was less outraged now, and his tone became avuncular as he told us about
boys in his classes, who, as young men, fell into bad company, and became
gamblers and drunkards. And maybe it started just with a few friends who
told filthy stories and used bad language, he added. I thought of my mates,
Herbie, Ernie, Charlie, Jim. I remained silent. They weren't bad company;
they were good company. And in saying nothing to Doot in defence of
them, I felt I had betrayed them. I half-wished he had caned me rather than
preached at me. There were no more jokes that afternoon.

On the next morning, I discovered that I was a celebrity. Nobody, so
far as anyone knew, had dared ever to tell a dirty joke in Doot's class. In
the bog, boys pitched my punchline to one another and whacked it with
a snigger, and asked me if I used Lifebuoy soap to wash my mouth out. I
enjoyed the fame but I knew that I had been naïve. And I knew I didn't like
Doot. Devout holy flipping Doot.

On May 8th 1945, the war in Europe ended. Hitler was dead, and it seemed
that our summer holidays began then. In that same month I turned twelve
years of age, the age at which Jesus had confounded the scholars in the
Temple. Neither Doot nor I were confounding anybody now. One morning
of the handful remaining in our year with him, Doot told us the story of
Belshazzar, a ghostly story, from the Book of Daniel.

Belshazzar, the king of the Babylonians, threw a great feast. The
Babylonians praised their gods and mocked the true God. Late in the evening
the king saw a disembodied hand writing on the palace wall. His legs turned
to jelly and his knees knocked while the hand wrote MENE, MENE, TEKEL,
UPHARSIN. He couldn't understand the words and so great was his fear

that he promised to reward whoever could interpret the writing. Nobody could, except Daniel, a captive Jew, who had a reputation for interpreting dreams. The writing meant: 'Thou art weighed in the balances and found wanting'. That night in Babylon Belshazzar was murdered.

Doot warned us against leaving repentance until it was too late. But in a sense other than Doot meant, the writing was on the wall for us.

We had begun to believe that because we had learned so little with Doot, we were going to find the next Standard – Sixth, which was Copey's class – hard. Doot hadn't pushed us to learn, we said. He had spent time on religion, and we wasted time by sidetracking him to the signs of the times and the end of the world.

Yet in his class I mastered the skill of elementary algebra, even to the point of becoming fond of it. I was fascinated with the little elementary science we did, with mercury darting capriciously on a tilting glass paten like molten lead, with the silver disk of light that floated on top of water in a test tube as we learned to measure metrically the volume of a penny and a sixpence, and with the charming set of scales on which we weighed small pieces of tarnished brass and thin dull squares of lead and tin. I drew his praise for my compositions despite my penmanship, for my writing had a backward slant, the tall consonants leaning like drunks leaving a pub 'two sheets to the wind'.

I was a 'clutey', left-handed, but Doot had never forced me to write with my right hand. Nor had any of my teachers, so far. My condition had its usefulness, for a 'clutey' could be tricky at bowling and batting in cricket. But at other times, you looked and felt awkward, footery. Old countrywomen called the Devil 'Old Clutey'.

IV

One afternoon in the autumn of the new school year – I was now in Sixth Standard, in Mr Copeland's class – I was summoned to Doot's classroom. My brother was now in his class, and I thought the summons had something to do with him.

Doot was agitated, and he had his cane in his hand. He led me to a window and pointed downward. I looked out. On the playground beneath the window someone had scrawled in thick limestone letters, an obscene four-lettered word, and beneath it, HOLY DOOT.

'Is that your work, Morrison?' he asked, his face dark with fury.

'No, sir,' I replied.

The implication in his question shook me.

'Are you telling me the truth?'

'Yes, sir.'

My face burned, and my stomach roiled, but I felt no shame. While I stood under the gaze of everyone in the class, Doot called for the offender to own up, and when nobody did, he hectored us all on the virtues of honour and honesty. Nobody confessed.

Doot dismissed me without another word. Confused, and now angry, I returned along the empty, silent corridor to Copey's class. The memory of how he had shamed me for my joke still smarted. Now Doot had been mocked. Good. But why had he assumed that I, whom he praised for my compositions, was the mocker, that my hand had traced the offending words on the playground? Yet, oddly, I felt disquieted, not quite innocent.

Later in the morning, in the bog, my mates were anxious to know why Doot had sent for me, and what had happened, and they whooped with glee when I told them, for I told them with relish, and we aimed our pee high up the wall, spattering the scrawls and scratches that defaced the brown brick.

'HOLY DOOT. That's a good'un. An' th' other word. Ye'd git kicked outa school for writin' that. Did ye really do it, Willie?'

'I didn't. Hanest.'

For a moment, I enjoyed the innuendo that I was capable of such an act of defiance and ridicule, and brave enough to do it.

'Doot'll always think ye did.'

'I know.'

We stormed out of the bog and raced to where the windows of Doot's classroom overlooked the playground. An attempt had been made to wash off the inscription but the limestone had left an imprint on the grey weathered concrete, which the boots of boys chasing a wee rubber ball would eventually erase, unlike the more indelible kind of writing.

The more I gave thought to the incident, the clearer I understood why it had upset Doot so much. In the end, Doot wasn't easy, but we couldn't hate him the way we hated Taylor. So we mocked him. The hand of the unknown, unholy scribe was the hand of everyone who had weighed Doot and found him wanting. And, I believe, he believed it too, for he was shaken.

But I found no satisfaction in that judgment.

Epilogue

After I left Everton school, I never saw any of my teachers again. Had I known them in my adult years I would have a different image of them than the blinkered, and perhaps unfair, image from my childhood. Together, they taught me, some more effectively than others, how to read and write, and do arithmetic, and reel off from memory the names of the counties of Ireland and shires of England and Scotland and Wales. Miss Hutchinson, Head Mistress of Senior Infants and my first teacher, taught me not to be ashamed of being left-handed. Mr Copeland, the Sixth Standard master, thought I had it in me to become a teacher, but my parents couldn't afford to keep me at school after the normal leaving age of fourteen.

I heard years later that Mr McCullough became a successful principal of a school on the Shankill Road, a tougher area of the city than Ardoyne, where Everton school was. No mean feat, and maybe it was because, after all, he loved teaching and genuinely cared about his pupils. As for his influence on me, well, therein is one of life's ironies.

In my early youth I was drawn to the teachings of the Plymouth Brethren and though I never fully embraced them I became as devout as any Plymouth Brother. Did Doot ever know that? But that's not the question I would have asked him, had we met in later years. I would have asked him why he thought I was the boy who publicly dared to mock him? Was it the slope of the hand? The answer is lost in the great silence.

Chapter 14

ON THE STREET

IN A small kitchen house, two is company, three's a crowd, and any more than that needs crowd control. If a squabble erupts, you have to read the Riot Act, and clear the kitchen. 'Out, out inta th' street, youse.' And so the four of us, my brother, two sisters and I, would find ourselves, not always unwillingly, sitting on the kerb of a footpath, which the Yanks call a 'sidewalk', waiting for a game to start, or just waiting.

It was a good spot to wait, at street level, because you could see everything that passed up and down the street: horse drawn carts, men in gabardine coats, and if it was a Sunday, men with greyhounds and gunny sacks that wriggled, other men with hurley sticks, children you didn't know, all of them from the district at the bottom of your street and parading up *your* street, Alliance Road, as if they owned it. The nerve of them!

You had to watch out for huge hairy hooves and creaking cart wheels that made you pull in your feet for fear of having your toes squashed. If the horse stopped beside you, you had to make yourself scarce and find a fresh spot: the horse might have a weak bladder. If it was a mare, you moved toward its head, if a stallion, toward its rear, where you ran the risk, however, that its bowel was overloaded. You never had to look out for motor cars; a motor car on the street was as rare as a docker coming home sober on a Friday night.

Several horse-drawn vehicles went up and down the street every day and over the space of a week. The first one arrived early in the morning, somewhere between six and seven, and so I rarely saw it, much less sat on the kerb waiting for it. I was usually in bed when it came along. If you slept lightly, you would hear the rattle of milk crates and creak of wheels, and a moment later the tinkle of bottles at your front door, when the milkman picked up empties, and you could go back to sleep knowing that there was milk for your porridge and tea. Or get up, if that was your inclination. It was never mine. I didn't like to get out of bed when the world was just beginning to scratch itself; it's catching.

In the summertime, when I had no school to run to for nine o'clock, my mother sometimes sent me out to the street wait for the bread server. Joe, the bread server, arrived somewhere between nine and ten o'clock. Of all the men who drove carts up and down our street week in and week out, he was the only one whose name I knew. He was popular because he was always on top of the world. The second he stopped his horse on the street he was besieged by women, who two hours earlier had ushered their men out to work with a kiss. You called your order, a plain loaf and two Paris buns, and waited, while Joe chatted up the women as he pulled out loaves and buns from the depths of the cart with a wooden 'hoe' the length of a billiard cue. Sometimes, Joe would let you feed his horse, hold the feed bag while the beast buried his nose in the oats or hay, lifted out a mouthful, chomped with huge teeth that would have crushed your hand if you weren't careful, and plunged back in again, until there was not a flake left in the bottom of the bag. Whereupon it shook its massive head vigorously, and snorted, whether in content or complaint, you never knew.

As the day moved with the sun, which was either bright or hidden behind a scowling sky, other carts would appear, depending on the day of the week. The grocery cart could show up on any day, but always did so on Friday, to deliver groceries to houses whose chatelaines wouldn't stoop to carry them from the shops – those who had 'a wire about themselves' we said, the pretentious ones with fancy curtains – or to folk who were too old or ill to run their own messages. Since it only stopped to make deliveries at certain houses, you could count on getting a bit of a ride on the back of the cart by hanging on to the tailboard as the horse trotted between its stops. A cranky carter would discourage free riders with a flick of his long whip backward over the cart and raise a welt across a pair of knuckles.

If your street was the last on his run, you were in luck. You followed the cart, and watched idly while he made his rounds, and as soon as he had delivered the last box of groceries, you loitered on the kerb behind the cart and pretended to look for a lost marble or sixpence. You waited until he was seated, had picked up the reins and whip, had clicked loudly or flicked his whip at the horse, before you stood up. At the first movement of the wheels, you grabbed hold of the tailboard, and because the tailboard had no bumper to rest your feet on, you had to pull your knees up until you were hanging in a hunker on the back of the cart.

The horse would be anxious to get back to the stable, and the driver to a pint of stout. The cart would tear down the street, the driver indifferent – if he noticed at all – to the pairs of small white knuckles gripping the tailboard as if they had been welded to it. You hung on for your dear life until the cart reached the bottom of the hill, where it had to slow down to turn into Alliance Avenue. At that spot you dragged your boots on the roadway to get the feel of the cart's momentum in preparation for letting go, for if you let go too soon you were thrown on the road, and would be lucky to leave nothing more on the street than a bit of skin from kneecaps and forearms. Once, when the cart was in full flight, a free-rider let go too soon, and an ambulance had to be summoned, and afterwards, somebody washed the bit of blood off the street.

Every Friday afternoon, between three and four o'clock, a nasal shout that ended in a bark echoed and re-echoed from down the street, 'Herrinsaloch!' 'Herrinsaloch!' Whether he was shouting, 'Herrings from the lough' or 'herrings a lot' I never knew, and never thought to ask him. Up you got off the kerb to run to your house to tell your mother that the herring man was coming. She would gave you a shilling and the basin from the scullery. The fish hawker, who always looked cold and pinched even on a summer's day, never stopped shouting while he pulled wet slippery herrings or mackerel out of boxes and dropped them into his customers' buckets, or wrapped them in newspapers. 'Six herrins, mister' you said, and six would plop into the basin, and you would drop the shilling into his wet scaly hand, and he would slide it into the throat of his sagging coat pocket. We ate herrings on Friday because they were always fresh off the boats. Mammy rolled them in flour and fried them or pickled them for Sunday's tea. My father wouldn't eat mackerel because, he said, they fed on the sea's shite.

If there is a pig god, I know what sort of incense pleases him. The slop cart, a big farmer's cart came around on Mondays or Tuesdays for the leftovers of our weekend feeding. You could smell the sweet sour of decomposing offal when the cart was a mile away from where you sat on the footpath. Elsewhere, in Derry for example, the fellow who collected slops was called 'the brockman'. We didn't have any name for him. A big broad man like Fatty Arbuckle, wrapped in an old gabardine coat the size of a blanket and piggin' filthy, and a duncher on his head, he filled the bench behind his horse, the reins in one hand and a whip in the other, and as pleased with himself at having a job no one else would do, like Winston Churchill. Now and again he uttered an inhuman gulder that started in the bottom of his lungs and exploded from the back of his throat to send shock waves along the street. If it was a word or phrase, it was so badly mangled as to be unrecognisable, but the meaning was clear enough. Doors would open here and there, and women would come out with their slop buckets.

He never got off the cart, but would point and grunt toward the place in the cart he wanted the women to throw their slops. He chewed tobacco, and from time to time, he would turn toward the ferment behind him, and send a shower of spit, like pellets from a large shotgun, into the middle of it. Now and again, he let you sit beside him for a while, if you didn't mind the smell of the cart, nor the smell of him. Every time his cart creaked up the street, I would remember the pigs at the farm in Loughgilly, to which I had been sent as an evacuee after the Blitz. Some boys vowed that when they grew up they would collect slops for pigs, but only God knows if any achieved his momentary heart's desire. No one I knew ever did.

Sitting on the kerb with nothing to do but stare at the sky behind the houses opposite, you begin to notice things that usually don't draw your attention when you are throwing yourself about the street in a game of football, in an exuberance of spirit at the expense of energy. Such as chimney pots. You know from the blackened and sometimes cracked state of the pot and the brick stack whose house had a chimney fire, who regularly set their chimneys on fire, and who never seemed to have had a chimney fire. You notice which chimneys smoke all the year around, and which sit dormant most of the day in the winter. Since without coal you would freeze to death in the winter, or at least catch pneumonia from the dampness – which, in some cases, led to the same end – one of the most important people to come to your street was the coal man.

The coal man came according to need, because the length of time a bag of coal lasted as fuel depended on the time of the year, the vicissitude of the weather, and whether you were like those persons who coddled themselves by burning big fires in their grates when the sun would be splitting the stones in July or August, which surprisingly, from time to time, it tried. He wore a leather apron beneath a short coat, like the jacket of a suit but of a coarser cloth, which had a sheen from years of coal dust. He would be boggin', black from the top of his duncher to the laces of his boots.

The fellow who most often delivered the coal to our house was small, but tough, a fact which gave me hope, for I was self-conscious about my small stature and light build. He would lean his back, which was covered with a sack as black as the coal, against the side of the cart, grab a bag of coal or slack – damp coal granules – by its ears, hump it on to his back, carry it, head craned forward, back bent, around to your yard behind your house and dump it in your coal box, if you had one.

You couldn't sit on the kerb and not want to help the coal man, and you would ask him if you could fold his empty sacks. If he didn't bark at you, but looked pleased with your offer, you asked him if you could ride beside him to his next customer or two. In for a penny, in for a pound, the sort of reasoning that in this case escaped a mother's understanding. If you were going to get filthy to your elbows with coal dust, and wipe the sweat off your face with the filthy back of your hand, then you might as well sit in it. We never rode on his tailboard. It wasn't worth the hammering you would get when you got home as filthy as the coal man, and not having the excuse that you were helping him. Sometimes, even that excuse didn't save you.

I couldn't name the breed of the horses that pulled these carts, but no matter, they were magnificent giants of creatures, even the old ones who pulled the carts as if every inch of street was a slog. You knew the unhappy one; it stood with its head hanging down. Now and again a horse was testy and the carter warned you to keep your distance, but for the most part, they stood patiently while you stroked their noses and flanks, and nickered if they felt like talking to you, or chewed their bits and whiffled through their huge lips if they didn't. And you wished you lived in the Wild West, where you could own a horse and not have to worry about where to keep it or how much dung it dropped.

They were manure machines. No sooner had a horse dropped a steaming golden or chocolate load on the street but somebody came out of a house, as if the place was on fire, to shovel it into a wee box. This had nothing to do with keeping the street clean, but everything to do with the wee gardens, with growing scallions that would reach the sky, and turnips as big as boulders, and roses that would make you blush as you passed them. Sometimes boys, and even men, almost came to blows with their shovels over who got to the pile first. If the steaming pile was right outside your house you believed you had rights to it.

The coal man and the pig man were, in different ways clarty, or dirty, but you didn't feel sorry for them. Nor for the bin men, who had a lorry, which moved up and down the street at a snail's pace while they emptied into it bins of ashes and refuse not fit for pigs. They were always in a clattering hurry, and you stayed out of their way. But there was one fellow you couldn't help pitying, whether or not he wanted, or needed, your pity.

You heard the ragman before you spotted him, a loud throaty yell that rose up through a curtain of catarrh, 'Reggs. Anyoul reggs.' Soon he followed the throw of his voice, and you would see him pushing his barrow boy's cart down the street. He looked as if he lived in a hedge. His long tattered overcoat and frayed duncher were in a worse state than the rags he was gathering, and hands that took your rags looked as if they had been unwashed since birth.

Among the rummage on his cart, he carried cups and saucers, bowls and plates and small pots, and if you fancied a bit of delph or tin, and thought your rags were worth more than the nothing he usually at first offered you, you would bargain with him. It wasn't exactly fun, because he could be testy, and the bargaining would become a barney, and he would swear at you. He was stubborn. My mother always thought him to be 'a poor lukin' craiter, but wi' no flies on 'im, mind you.' You didn't always get what you wanted for your castoffs. God knows, for all we knew he might have been a rich man, or at least, better off than anybody on our street. Sometimes he parked his cart at a street corner and plodded down the back field behind our house, crying his presence, and women would dicker with him over their wire fences.

. Another 'poor craiter' visited our street from time to time, an old fellow who sharpened knives and scissors. He wore glasses with thick lenses, and an old .gabardine that hung open from his shoulders and almost dragged on the ground. He pushed a contraption on wheels like an old-fashioned sewing machine, but had a large grindstone instead of a stitcher. As he trod the treadle to spin the grindstone, he leaned over until his nose was almost touching the spinning stone as if he was honing it too. 'He's just oilin' th' stone,' a wag once explained, because he often, like the ragman and other 'poor lukin' craiters', had a dripping nose and no hanky. My mother sometimes had him sharpen the kitchen knife or scissors, even if she thought that they were sharp enough. He charged what he could, and took what he got.

One fellow who got you off the kerb in a hurry was the ice-cream man. As soon as you spotted him puffing his cart up the hill, you charged home to cadge the price of a 'slider', an ice-cream sandwich, or a 'poke', which according to the comics English boarding school boys called a 'cornet'. He was a small fat Italian. He came from nowhere – that is from far away, at least once each summer week. Italians made the best ice-cream, we believed, even during the war when good ice cream was scarce because sugar was rationed. If you had no luck prying a penny or two from your mother, or of finding her purse if she was out, you could take out your frustration on the Italian, for until 1944 we were at war with Italy. We would shout 'Tallyumpazoo', or something like that, and he would gesticulate wildly, yell in Italian, and make a run at us. He never caught any of us, and so, we never knew what he would do to his tormentor. If he was a mystery, the word we hurled was a greater one. We thought it was Italian for the infamous four-lettered word. Maybe he, not speaking English well, thought it was a sinister or foul English word. Whatever the meaning, he heard it as an insult, and gave chase, which, we concluded, was not as good as his ice-cream.

From time to time, and they were anxious or sad times, the appearance of certain vehicles on the street always drew a crowd that started with one or two kerb-sitters with hearing like a sheep dog's, and soon swelled into an unwashed army of children from neighbouring streets as well as your own, who abandoned homework, games, and fighting with their siblings, to chase with craning necks these vehicles to their destinations.

The ambulance, its bell clanging to clear its way, was the only motorised vehicle that came up the street, except for the odd taxi with a huge gas bag on top, petrol being in short supply during the war. When the bell stopped ringing you knew it had arrived, and when you caught up with it, a hush had already fallen on the growing crowd, and was fanning out like an invisible gas to envelop latecomers, whose clatter of running feet died off into a respectful silence.

The hush wasn't solid; underneath it you could hear the whisperings of the curious and the guessers: 'Who's it?' 'Is't an oul man or oul woman or a wee chile?' 'Is he badly hurted or dead?' And so on. Younger was more exciting, because you expected the old to take sick. When a stretcher was taken out of the ambulance, you could feel the tension rise around you. 'Muss be bad, poor craiter.' Or, 'God love 'im, poor wee chile.' You craned your neck to see if the body was near death's door, which you could tell by the pallor of the skin and the glaze of the eyes, or already dead, in which case the head would be covered. You looked for bloody bandages too, and if there were any, the whisperings became a buzz and the hush floated off like a kite connected only by a thin string to the scene of suffering below. And if the patient walked out of the house to the ambulance, everybody felt let down and had wasted their time, and the whispers would become chatter. The hush would lift as if a cloud had puffed its cheeks and blew it away.

An ambulance was sent once for me. I had scarlet fever, and in having to walk to the ambulance instead of being carried on a stretcher like a wounded soldier, I was more disappointed than the crowd which was looking for the bloody bandages.

On the Street

A different sort of hush settled over a house where a hearse hitched to magnificent pair of black horses stood. The drawn window-blinds on the neighbouring house had already created a funereal atmosphere before the same crowd of small fry, augmented this time with more women, would gather. Nobody dared to talk at the solemn moment when the coffin entered the street feet first from the house, but everybody's thoughts must have mounted to a pile of pennies, if not half-crowns. If the funeral was for a child, which, sadly, was the case from time to time, or of someone in his or her prime who was leaving little children orphans, all the women around you would be weeping as if they were at the foot of the Cross, and you felt a sadness hanging like a heavy chain from your heart. You didn't sit on the kerb to watch a funeral. That was rude, as disrespectful as spitting as you passed a church. You stood, and doffed your skullcap as it passed. And after the last man in the cortege was well out of sight, you took your time about starting a game, or went back to your kerb to shuffle your feet aimlessly in the gutter.

All of us fancied being telegram boys, if we couldn't be coal men or pig men. You got a belt with a pouch and a pill box hat with a chin strap, and a bike and bicycle clips, though they weren't much use when you wore short trousers. An older boy who lived next door to me became one, and we envied him 'til we were as green as our garden grass.

When a telegram boy's bicycle nosed up over the lower hill of our street during the war years, you could feel the street trembling from where you were sitting on the kerb. Not many women on our street had husbands or sons in the Army or Air Force or Navy. You knew that if they saw the telegram boy, their hearts would stop until he passed. Sometimes, the telegram had nothing to do with the war, but when it did, it was a shock to the neighbours of the woman who got it, but that was little compared to her grief.

One night, the eleventh of July, 1945, the war in Europe having ended in May but the Japanese and Allies still at it in the Pacific, a telegram boy arrived on our part of the street early one evening. I didn't notice him, because I was sitting on the kerb with a bunch of cronies at the bonefire we had built from old furniture, wooden boxes, and branches we had hacked from trees up the Ardoyne Loney. The fire was roaring in the summer twilight, and we were belting out Orange songs. I felt a tap on my shoulder. It was my mother. 'Get youse home,' she said in a severe voice to Norman and me. I thought, 'What've we done nigh?' When we were in the house, she told us that Mrs McNalley, who lived next door to us, on the other side of us from the Hynes, had just received a telegram informing her that her husband, a Merchant Navy seaman, had been lost at sea in the Pacific Ocean. The McNalleys were Roman Catholics. We didn't go back to the bonfire. And we didn't watch the Orangemen walk that year.

What about the men in gabardine coats, you ask? Ah, yes. Well, I was coming to them. From where you sat on the kerb, you could see them coming from either direction, down the hill or up the street, coat buttoned, clean, paddy hat on head and maybe a cigarette in the mouth. They came early in the week, book in hand from house to house, before what was left of the wages after the weekend spree dissipated in further prodigalities: the rent man every Monday, and every Tuesday the insurance man. You watched to see who let him into her house, and how long he stayed, and who made him stand at the door stoop, and who slammed the door after he left.

Now and again the woman from the Welfare Council appeared without warning, and the word of her whereabouts would be passed along the street, as if invisible tom toms beat out the alarm. There would be a sudden frenzy in the houses of floor-washing and tidying and making sure the bath tub upstairs showed no sign of doubling as a coal box.

Only the appearance of the Presbyterian minister or the Church of Ireland parson caused such a disruption of daily life, and then only among those of their persuasion. Agnostics and atheists were spared. My mother, on hearing that the minister was on the street, would order us to hide our comics under the cushions of the chairs, and to wipe our faces and knees in preparation for the customary prayer, led by the minister standing at the mantelpiece, his back to the fire, us kneeling at the chairs.

You could tell the difference between a Protestant and Catholic clergyman by the size of the white collar he wore back to front. The Protestant's collar was like a white bandage around the neck, the Catholic's like an inch of white cardboard tucked into the neck of his black shirt. If you still had a doubt, because some priests wore the wide collar, you looked at the clergyman's coat lapel to see it had a Pioneer badge. Priests were usually death against strong drink, and so were Protestant ministers, but they didn't wear a badge to warn you. Although there were a few Catholic families on the street, you rarely saw a priest, and when you did, you sat where you were until he passed. Not so with nuns. Once you spotted a pair – they were always in pairs – rising over the hill like two blackbirds, you got to your feet, and moved across the road to the kerb on the other side, in case their shadow might fall on you and bring you bad luck.

We didn't sit much on the kerb at weekends. On those days, the street took on the life of a thoroughfare – a 'road' proper – for people on foot on their way from the claustrophobic streets around Ewart's Mill to the expanse of fields that opened out at the top of our street. Beyond these fields, to the north lay the heather uplands of Squires Hill, and to the east the route to Cave Hill and Napoleon's Nose, from which you had a magnificent panorama of Belfast Lough stretching out toward the Irish Sea, of the Holywood Hills on the far side of the Lough, of the city, and of Queen's Island, the shipyards at the mouth of the River Lagan.

On Sunday afternoon especially, you could spend an interesting hour or two standing at your garden gate to watch the motley parade of men in scarves and dunchers, with muzzled lean starved-looking greyhounds at their heels, on their way to the fields, where they trained them for the Dog Races at the Duncairn or Celtic Park. Some men carried ferrets in gunny sacks. The ferrets flushed rabbits out of their holes in the fields for the greyhounds to chase. Other men carried hurley sticks. The Catholics were mad about hurley, and the wide open spaces at the top of our street gave them a lot of room to smack the hurley ball hard and far while greyhounds raced about their feet.

Now and again, you would get a nod from one of the men, and you would nod back, for nodding costs nothing whatever your religion. Sometimes in the summer, when we had no Sunday school to go to in the afternoon, we would follow them 'up th' fields' as we would say, to watch the unmuzzled dogs racing in circles and crazy figures-of-eight after an unfortunate rabbit.

In fine weather, children in pairs or small bands from the lower end tramped up the street on their way in April and May to gather primroses, and in summer, bluebells, and you would see them coming back down the street later in the day, pink faced and sore of foot, pleased as punch with fists and arms full of paradise, and all for their mammies, and to brighten for a while their dark kitchens and bedrooms. You knew how they felt, for on many a Saturday and Sunday afternoon you left the kerb to scour the hedgerows along the Horseshoe Road and Carr's Glen beyond, and return with your own share of glory, and in time for a tea of salad and sponge cake.

By the late 1940s horse-drawn hearses had finally left the streets and their place taken by the less splendid Rolls Royce, or motors of that class. Electric-driven vans replaced the milk and bread carts. The coal man and the fish hawker each got lorries. For a while the slops cart alone trundled up the street, and by the end of the decade it too disappeared, together with the rag man, who probably moved to a villa in Portugal, and Tallyumpazoo, who probably opened a fancy Italian ice-cream emporium.

And by that time too, I had abandoned forever my place on the kerb.

Epilogue

During the summer of 1989, I made my last visit to the street. It was brief and I didn't get out of the car. Strangers now lived in the house where I grew up, and latest models of cars lined the street tightly against the footpaths.

There was no room for a boy to sit on the kerb.

Chapter 15

REMAINS

TWO DAYS after our next-door neighbour said she smelled funeral flowers in our house, my Granda Porter dropped dead. And she had a fit of hysterics, for she believed that her words had cursed him. I remember the time well, but not mainly because of what she said. At the time I paid no attention to it, for nobody in our family was dead. Not yet.

I was eleven, going on twelve years. I hadn't been at school that February morning, because I had wheezed and coughed during the night. Outside the damp air was chill enough to draw a drip to the nose, and Mammy, afraid that I might have another attack of bronchitis – I had a weak chest, she said, though I could run the legs off most boys my age – thought I should stay at home for the day. Our wee kitchen, where as the need arose we ate, loafed, played, read, or received visitors – for we had no parlour – was warm and smelled faintly of the menthol of Vick's Chest Ointment. In the grate a fire banked up with coal slack simmered, sending a thin curtain of pale blue smoke up the chimney. I sat cross-legged on the floor close to the fire, carving with a penknife a small block of wood into the slender fuselage of a Spitfire fighter. The parings fell among fine silvery ash spilling softly from time to time between the bars of the grate and onto the hearth. In the scullery off the kitchen Mammy fistled among the breakfast dishes. A BBC voice murmured on the wireless.

The morning was at ease with itself. But not for long.

Our door knocker rattled in a familiar rhythm that ended in two decisive raps. I opened the door to Joe, the insurance man. Mammy, coming in to the kitchen from the scullery, instantly picked up the black, bent poker from the hearth and thumped it three times on the wall dividing our house from our neighbour's. Then she turned off the wireless. Joe stepped into the kitchen.

'Hallo, Mabel. That's a brave day. Bit of a nip in th' air.'

Mammy replied with a question:

'Wee cup of tea in yer han', Joe?'

Without waiting for his answer, she returned to the scullery.

On his weekly round to collect insurance premiums Joe always stopped at our house long enough for a smoke and cup of tea. He took off his hat, opened his raincoat, sat down at the table, and pulled out his insurance book and a packet of cigarettes. Mammy had bought a penny policy from the company he represented, the Prudential Insurance Co., or the 'Prue'. 'To pay for funerals,' she had said.

The morning stirred.

Joe was a *quare geg,* fond of a good pint, and a fierce curser. He could make a great yarn about his Saturday night at the pub, gild the gossip he picked up on his rounds, about who was getting a 'wee squeeze' while her man was at work. For years he had been the local bread server. In fair and foul weather he drove his bread cart up our street every weekday morning, stopping every few yards. Doors of houses opened and women, turbaned or bristling with curling pins, housecoats clinched with one arm or pinnies drawn tight around their breasts, shuffled or flapped in fur-trimmed carpet slippers down their brief garden paths, gathered around the cart and shouted their orders, as he pulled from dark recess of his cart, trays of loaves and buns.

Mammy sent me out to the cart sometimes, for a loaf or a barmbrack and maybe, if she could afford them, big cream buns. When Joe opened the back doors of the cart and pulled out the trays of loaves, a warm smell of fresh bread poured into the street, and you wanted to bask in it all morning. Occasionally, the horse took advantage of the stop and pished. Joe cursed the beast, and the hot stink of urine circled the cart, swallowing up the smell of the bread for a few minutes.

Joe gave up the bread cart. The early hours in bad weather got him down, he said. We thought we would miss him, but he didn't disappear from our street. He turned up with an insurance book.

A minute or two after Joe had settled himself in our kitchen, Mrs Hynes,

Mammy's neighbour and good friend, let herself into our house. A draught of cold air raced round the kitchen floor, brushing my knees where I sat. Even though she had lived next door since before the war and one of her two sons was my best friend, I never called her by her Christian name, 'Vi'. Her husband, whom we rarely saw, was a soldier, stationed for most of the war in England. A thin woman, she wore her pinny like a second skin, so tightly did she wrap it around her. Although a fussy housekeeper, she found time to sit for hours in her kitchen with a paperback romance or *True Confessions* magazine in one hand and a feg in the other, her marbled shins almost up against the bars of the grate. So Mammy said. Mammy, who was neither skinny nor fat, nor a smoker, didn't read much more than the Sunday newspapers and *The Belfast Telegraph*, mostly the death notices on the inside of the front page which she read aloud to us if she knew the dead person's family: 'McNeely, Jack. January 16th 1945, suddenly. Dearly beloved husband of Sadie, and father of (and here she read out a list of names) and grandfather of (and another list of names). Remains will be removed to Carnmoney Cemetery for burial. Deeply regretted. Gone but not forgotten.'

The Catholic notices gave me the goose bumps I always felt when I heard Paul Robeson sing 'Ole Black Joe' on one of Mammy's gramophone records. They always ended: 'On his soul, sweet Jesus, have mercy', for Catholics believed in purgatory and so remained unsure about whether their loved one would make it to Heaven. That seemed to me a double grief.

But sometimes I wondered what it would be like to read a death notice about somebody in your own family, and have your name listed under 'Deeply regretted by...'

Mrs Hynes spoke to Joe:

'You're lukin' quare'n'good, Joe. Not doin' ye any harm, th' insurance, so it's not.'

'Better than sittin' behind a fartin' horse, Vi.'

We all laughed. And she said to me with a wee laugh,

'Mitchin' school th'day, Will?'

Mammy explained, and Mrs Hynes looked sympathetic. She pulled her Woodbines from her pinny pocket, and was about to light up but sniffed:

'There's a smell of funeral flowers in yur house, so there is, Mabel.'

'It's Will's chest rub ye smell, Vi. It's in his jersey.'

'No, I smell flowers, Mabel, so I do.'

She sniffed again. Joe laughed:

'Ye putting the jinx on me, Vi? Bejesus, ye'll be havin' me goan back on th' bloody cart.'

He flicked ash into the hearth. Mrs Hynes lit her Woodbine from his, and soon the wee kitchen, and my jersey, reeked with the smell of tobacco.

Before long the tears were tripping us, as Mammy always said about laughs that hurt your ribs. She and Mrs Hynes had a tooth for a good story and Joe gave them plenty to chew on. From time to time Mammy glanced at me to see if I laughed at the bits of his stories about the squeezes. I kept a straight face, but I knew what was going on. Still, I had a good laugh too, mainly at his cursing. He was the worst curser I had ever heard; so bad, in fact, that I often wondered why God hadn't struck him dead for taking a whole host of holy names in vain.

Joe told stories better than the comedians at the Empire Theatre where Mammy and Daddy took my brother, sisters, and me one year just after Christmas. He had a hoarse smoker's voice, and he would get excited as he told his stories, his cigarette weaving blue and white trails in the air, and he would gallop toward the finishing post where he would collapse into laughter and a fit of coughing, Mammy and Mrs Hynes all the while laughing with him and rocking back and forth on their chairs, as if their bellies ached. After Joe left they had another good laugh between themselves, putting their own twist on his tales, and getting another mile out of the story about him having 'to crack me whip agin an entry wall'. The crack about the flowers was forgotten. Until two days later.

When I came home from school that afternoon, I had found Mammy sitting at the kitchen table, the tears tripping her, and they weren't the kind that come from laughing, although there were two cups and a plate of raisin bread on the table. She was heart-scalded. I had seen her in this state before, but at those times she had been playing records of hymns on our wind-up gramophone: 'Rock of ages cleft for me', or 'Shall we gather at the river' or 'When the roll is called up yonder, I'll be there'. The voices always sounded as if the singers' noses were stuffed with catarrh.

Mammy wasn't a religious woman, though she would go to church sometimes on Sunday evening if she heard that the visiting preacher was a good storyteller. When from time to time I got saved at the wee Friday night meeting in the Ardglen Mission Hall at the bottom of our street, and told her because we were told you couldn't keep it a secret or you wouldn't stay saved, she would say, 'You'll be gettin' religious mania.' She was a bit cynical about religion. My Grandma Porter, who had died of throat cancer when I was four, had been very religious, but Mammy loved her. She said that Grandma was a lovely women, kind and gentle, and so, when she grieved sore for her she would play Grandma's records and have a good cry. This time I didn't hear music, and I knew something was wrong.

'Yur Granda Porter dropped dead this morning on th' Oldpark Road, son,' she said, and she told me how she knew.

A friend, who lived near my Granda, had brought the bad news just after lunch-time. We had no telephone, and so news, whether good or bad, came by post, telegram, or in person. Mammy thought Mrs McChesney was just up for a wee visit, for she hadn't seen her in a while. She put the teapot on, and cut some slices off a raisin loaf. 'I knew something was wrong,' Mammy said, 'for she was fidgety until I sat myself down with me cup of tea.'

Granda had been shopping, and had collapsed outside the butcher's shop on Oldpark Road in the district we called 'The Bone'. A quick-witted woman among the small crowd that had quickly gathered called out:

'Has any of youse any whiskey or brandy?'

Somebody came out of the pub at the corner of the street with whiskey in a tumbler, and she poured some into my Granda. Had he known what was happening he would have enjoyed that, for he was fond of the drink. But he was too far gone for the whiskey to do him any good. The butcher telephoned for an ambulance, and then sent his assistant to tell Mrs McChesney who lived near the shop, for he knew that she knew Mammy.

When Mrs McChesney left, and Mammy had some time to herself to take in the bad news, she had rapped on the wall with the poker, she said.

In came Mrs Hynes, expecting a mouthful of tea and a wee chat. When she saw the state of Mammy's face and heard about Granda, she had a fit of hysterics. Mammy had spent the first half hour of her own sorrow calming her down, assuring her that there was no connection between the crack about the flowers and my Granda's death, and that she didn't blame her. Mammy wasn't a superstitious woman.

I didn't know what to say or do, but before I had time to think about what I should do, Mrs Hynes came in and took me into her house where my brother and sisters were already sitting quietly on her sofa, as bewildered as I was with this sudden strange interruption of our ordinary lives. She told us in a nice way to be good children because our Mammy was heart-scalded, losing her father so sudden like that. We sat on the sofa as if we were glued to it, whispering among ourselves or staring at her spotless shining oilcloth, and waited for the unfolding of whatever would unfold. Before the day was out, Mrs Hynes had taken charge of our house.

At tea-time she sent us home. Daddy was now back from the shipyard. After we had our tea, Mammy rapped on the wall with the poker, and in came Mrs Hynes. And the bustle began.

First, it had to be decided where my grandfather's body would lie until the day of the funeral. Our house had only two bedrooms upstairs, and downstairs a kitchen, scullery, and a wee room you couldn't swing a cat in. My father and mother slept in the back bedroom, which looked out into the back yard and over the field behind the house, and my brother, sisters and I slept in the front bedroom, which looked over our small garden on to the street. It had two beds; a small one in which my brother and I slept, and a big one with a mattress stuffed with some sort of minced cloth which used to ooze out of rips in the tick. At one time all of us slept in it, but now only my sisters did. Sometimes people laid the coffin in the kitchen, underneath the window, so that the dead person was always part of all the fuss of funerals. You were always half-waiting for the body in the coffin to butt into the talk, or to correct anything you said about him, or have a wee laugh to himself, or sit up and ask for a cup of tea and a biscuit, or in my Granda's case, a pint of Guinness. Mammy quite sensibly thought that the back bedroom would be the best room for the coffin. For the 'dead' room.

With the bedrooms reduced to one, Mammy decided that my brother and sisters, who were younger than me, would sleep at the neighbours, and I would sleep in the big bed in the other bedroom with my uncle John, Mammy's youngest brother, who was about twenty-two years old and lived with my Granda but had come to stay with us now, and Daddy and Mammy would sleep downstairs on the sofa and armchairs.

Mrs Hynes set to work to prepare the room for the coffin. The bed and dresser were taken out, the oilcloth scrubbed and polished, and a wee mat laid in the middle of the floor. A low fancy table and a vase for flowers was set at the window which looked out into the back yard. Two kitchen chairs were set against the wall opposite the one where the coffin would lie, and an armchair in one corner. Mammy thought that Mrs Hynes had made the room just lovely. She said to me, 'Will, wouldn't it be nice to keep it like this always?' 'It would, Mammy,' I said, thinking it would be a nice wee room to read in, when it was no longer the 'dead' room. And thinking she meant it, I wondered where she and Daddy would sleep.

After Mrs Hynes had swept our house from top to bottom, we sat on the sofa waiting for unfamiliar events to unfold. Had Granda died in our house, some of our neighbours would have washed him and laid him out on a bed just as if he was asleep. Then, the undertakers would come from Willie Wilton's Funeral Home with an empty coffin and put him in it. Because he had died on the street from a heart attack, his body had been taken to a hospital. So, we had to wait until the next day for the coffin with him in it.

That night I kept awakening out of my sleep. I had felt quite grown-up when I was told that I would be sleeping at home and not with Herbie next door, even if he was my best friend. But I didn't like the thought of sleeping next door to the 'dead' room, even if my uncle slept beside me. I kept my fear to myself; I wouldn't let anyone think I was not as brave as adults seemed to be with a dead person lying around.

To distract myself I played word games. On the wall above the foot of the big bed there hung a framed text in old-fashioned blue coloured letters like those on Christmas cards: BUT GOD COMMENDETH HIS LOVE TOWARD US, IN THAT, WHILE WE WERE YET SINNERS, CHRIST DIED FOR US. Romans 5:8. I only understood the part of the text about 'sinners' and Christ dying for us, because we learned that stuff in Sunday school. When I couldn't sleep and didn't have a comic to read by the light from the landing at the top of the stairs, I used to see how many words I could find in words like COMMENDETH and SINNERS and CHRIST. But that night I couldn't concentrate on it. I thought hard about the word LOVE, but I couldn't twist it into any other word that made sense. My mind kept flitting back to people I knew who had died.

My first school chum, Sandy. Dead from pneumonia, and only six. Now I've lived to be twice his age. Two boys in my class at Everton School killed in the air raids – so the teacher said. Stevie Foster, who I used to sit beside in school. He was skinny like me, and a good runner. He was only eleven years old when he fell to his death trying to climb a sheer sixty-foot rock face from the first to the second cave on Cave Hill. My Grandma Porter had died when I was four years old. I couldn't remember her clearly; only as a shadow bending over me when Mammy cut off all my curls. But I could still see the dark at the top of the stairs in her gas-lit house, and the strangely quiet shadows of women gliding up and down the stairs. And here it was all again, in our house. The dark, the shadows, the queer quietness. I was older now, but I was scared.

A death in the family was not like knowing people who had died. It was like – well, I didn't know, except that it was different.

The next morning the narrow polished oak coffin arrived, and was carried upstairs, and opened. I felt a little ashamed of my fear, because Granda Porter and I had been good friends. I often visited him in the afternoons, when I came home from school. He and my uncle John lived in a row house even smaller than ours in Ballymena Street, opposite the Sacred Heart Roman Catholic Church. A small wiry man, he had been a boilermaker's helper in the shipyard, and when he retired he had kept himself busy tailoring coats and trousers for neighbours. He was lucky he had lived so long because one night during the Troubles in the '20s, so Mammy told me, he and a mate came out of the pub at the corner of his street and were having a yarn when his mate fell dead, shot by a sniper firing a chance from the Catholic side of the Bone. And he was nearly killed in the Blitz.

Often when I visited him I would find him seated cross-legged on his gate-legged table, which had been pushed up against the window to give him better light. With his thick fingers he threaded his needle and neatly stitched and sewed. Sometimes, he would ask me to thread the needle for him. I would wet the end of the thread, hold the needle up to the light from the window, and guide the thread through the tiny eye. I had good eyes, but sometimes I had to try two or three times, because the point of the thread would bend at the needle's eye. Mammy said Granda was better than some of the tailors in the shops downtown.

He always made me a cup of tea on the kitchen range. It took up most of one wall. Above it, a sooty chimney flue, wide enough for a boy chimney sweep to get his head and shoulders into, disappeared upwards into darkness. The oven and grate were as black as crow's feathers, because Granda regularly blackened it with a brush and a sort of shoe polish. The half-round silver edging round the range, and the silver fender around the hearth gleamed, sometimes with a rosy colour from the glowing coals, and sometimes a yellow-blue from flames flickering between the bars of the grate. Every night he swept up the ashes in his hearth before he went to bed.

We sat at each end of this range, he in his armchair and I on a leather pouffe, drinking tea. He drank from a small white bowl with blue rings around it, or supped the tea from a saucer, I, from a smaller one. And we talked about my school, and Alliance Road, and this and that, and let the heat from the fire warm our faces and shins. Uncle John played the mouth organ, and sometimes, when he was there, he would play, and I would sing, and Granda would sew away at a pair of trousers. One day, I started to sing 'The Sash', and he stopped me, and said I wasn't to sing that kind of song in his house. I never asked him why not, and now it's too late to know.

All day long a steady creak of people went up and down the stairs to the wee room where my Granda lay. Friends, neighbours. Joe the insurance man dropped in. In the evening uncles and aunts and cousins of Mammy's – Doyles and Porters I had never seen before – stood and sat about the kitchen, and upstairs. I knew Uncle Joe Doyle, who was a soldier and a powerful drinker, and we had to keep an eye on him, Mammy said, for he would have already been to the pub before he arrived at our house. I met my great-uncle Stanley Porter for the first time in my memory, although he might have seen me as a baby or a wee child. He owned 'S. Porter Ltd.', the biggest news agents in Belfast, and lived in the swanky part of the city, and he gave me half-a-crown as he was leaving. Mammy told me that he had started his business with just a handcart, which he pushed piled with newspapers and magazines from the docks to tobacconist and sweetie shops around town.

I was dressed in my Sunday clothes: a white shirt and good Sunday grey trousers, a grey pullover and a tie with narrow blue and black stripes, grey socks that came up to my knees, with blue bands around their tops, and black shoes. I would rather have worn my boots, because I was fond of them, but boots were not suitable for a funeral. All the men wore black ties, and the women black dresses. The women looked nice in their dresses, especially Mammy.

Women jammed the wee scullery, washing cups and saucers, making tea and sandwiches; egg and onion, tomato and lettuce, ham, and tinned salmon. You could eat as many as you wanted, and nobody told you not to stuff yourself. You could eat your fill of fancy and plain biscuits and wee buns, and nobody spoiled it by telling you that you would get sick and would have to swallow Castor Oil. But, still, you minded your manners, and didn't speak unless spoken to.

The house was full of flowers, lilies and chrysanthemums, and others whose names I didn't know. They had been arriving all morning, and a lot of them were put beside the coffin. The blinds were always partly down in every room. But the lights were kept on all day, and a fire burned in the grate. Daylight poured into the hall every time someone came or went. Yet the house felt dim. Shadows flitting up and down the stairs, hovering about the landing. Some of the women always looked red-eyed. I could understand Mammy weeping, because Granda was her father. People spoke quietly to her, but when the men talked together they were loud, and now and again somebody laughed. I didn't pay attention to what they were saying, because most of the time I had my nose stuck in a library book.

At teatime, *The Belfast Telegraph* fell through the letterbox. I picked it up and opened it to the inside of the front page. Births, Marriages, Deaths. I ran my finger down the list. Yes, there, 'Porter, James, beloved husband of the late… Deeply regretted by…' I looked for my name. There, '… grandchildren…' Unnamed.

I opened the front door to breathe in the cool air from outside. The day had worn down to raw darkness.

Late at night the clatter of cups and saucers ceased in the scullery, and the house became still. The hearth was a mess of cigarette- and coal ash. Most of the callers had gone, and it was time for me to go to bed. I stood for a minute or so at the bottom of the stairs looking up. A dim light hung from the ceiling above the landing. I should have asked Mammy if the door of her bedroom was closed, but I didn't want to show that I was nervous. My heart hammered, and I thought it would burst itself against my chest. I could hardly breathe. When I was close to the top of the stairs, I peeped around the corner of the landing to make sure that the door to the 'dead' room was closed. Then I slipped into the bathroom, emptied my bladder for it had filled up with tea, and tiptoed into the bedroom without looking directly at the closed door, although I couldn't escape noticing it as I passed. My bed was cold, and so I bunched myself into a wee ball, and fell asleep.

In the 'dead' room, Granda sat up in his coffin.

I screamed, but no one heard me. My uncle was not in bed beside me. The landing light was on. I sat up, shivering, and realised that I had only screamed in my dream. Now I was wide awake. In the low light, the blue letters in the black framed text hanging on the wall above the foot of the bed looked black. Enough, I said to myself. I've had enough of this fear. I got out of bed and walked across the cold oilcloth to the landing. I could hear murmurs coming from the kitchen below. At the small bedroom I slowly opened the door. Light from the landing rushed into the room, thinning out the gloom. Holding the door handle as tightly as I held my breath, I peered into the room. A thick scent of flowers rushed up my nose, and I could feel my chest tighten. The coffin lay in shadow, and no one was sitting in it. I let go of the door handle, and switched on the light. My Granda never blinked. Just slept on.

His head lay on a little pillow, and someone had put a gauze covering over the coffin. I could still see him clearly, but the gauze made him look really dead, ghostly. I felt queasy, but I had decided that I would take a good long look at him, unlike the other times during the day when I just quickly glanced his way. I thought that if I did that, I would stop being scared of the dead. So, I studied this small still figure in its coffin.

He was, and yet he wasn't anymore, my Granda. Death had done something more to him besides stopping his heart, and taking away his breath. His pale face told me nothing. His thick white short hair, that always stood up, was neatly combed, and his eyebrows above his closed eyelids looked like smears of ashes. And his lips were shut tightly, as if he was wetting the end of a thread. He was dressed for church, in his navy blue suit and white shirt and tie, except that he never went to church, except for a wedding. And his hands lay on top of one another on his stomach, as if he had just had a good dinner. The white lining of the coffin felt soft. So much white, except for the dark coat and black tie. I felt odd to be looking down on him lying there. He looked smaller than he really was alive; almost as small as me. But I was not dead. He was, yet I couldn't think what it was that made him seem dead, apart from the fact that he wasn't breathing.

What does death really do to you?

I shivered, but now only from the cold. I switched off the light, quietly closed the door, and went back to bed, my mind trying to grasp something about Granda that lay out of the reach of words.

After that, the house lost its gloaming and the shadows faded away. I awakened to streaks of light behind the window-blind, and to the warmth of my uncle's back next to mine. In the daylight, the letters of the text on the wall had changed back to their blue colour. Downstairs in the kitchen the fire glowed, and throughout the day, the comings and goings continued.

From time to time I went upstairs to the small room, and milled among the visitors. My Granda's head was propped up now on the wee pillow. In spite of the fragrance of the flowers, I noticed a faint sweet odour I had never smelled before. It wasn't floor polish.

The next morning, near the time the funeral was to start, people filled our house and spilled on to the path and into the front garden. Some neighbours and my mates had gathered at the garden gate. Mammy and Daddy and Uncle John and the undertakers were upstairs. I stayed in the kitchen with my uncles and aunts. Voices were low and quiet, and everyone seemed to be waiting. There was a sadness in the house unlike the sadness of the days just past.

Then a loud voice from the street broke into the quietness:

'Here's th' Presbyterian minister.'

The message passed through the house quietly, as if borne on shoulders, up the stairs, into the scullery:

'Th' Rev. Mr Clements is here.'

At that, the sadness seemed to deepen. The minister came in, and mingled among us, shaking hands and nodding, speaking to Mammy and Daddy. I shrank into the corner beside the fireplace, where we kept our wireless. After a while, the minister's loud deep voice that always sounded a bit hoarse, rose out of the midst of the crowd in our kitchen, and the murmuring of voices died:

"Let not your heart be troubled. You believe in God, believe also in me. In my Father's house there are many mansions. If it were not so, I would have told you. I go to prepare a place for you."

He read other passages for the Bible that I had heard in church and at Sunday school. I tried to imagine a place of many mansions, and God wiping away all tears. and no more death, neither sorrow nor crying. The minister prayed, and at the 'Amen', I put on my overcoat and skull cap, and went into the street.

The damp cold felt good on my face. Overhead clouds had closed out the sky, but no rain had fallen. Blinds were drawn fully down the windows of nearby houses out of respect for the dead. Further down the street the blinds were only half-drawn. Women and children watched from their doorways. The undertakers set up two trestles on the pavement and went back inside the house. The street was silent, except for the odd snort or stamp of one of the black horses in front of the hearse. Then I heard the shuffle of uneven footsteps on the stairs, and whispers stirred among the spectators:

'They're bringin' him out nigh.'

'Youse wee childer stay away from the dur,' somebody cautioned, as the coffin, its narrow end first, emerged into the street.

The undertakers laid it on the trestles. I knew the crowd would be curious to see who had the first lift and who would be first lined up behind the coffin. The house emptied, the men trickling down the footpath, the women, Mammy among them, bunched together, arms around each other, at the garden gate. The undertakers lifted the coffin on to the shoulders of my Daddy and Uncle John and two of Mammy's cousins. They had their arms across each other's shoulder, as if they were getting their picture taken or singing a duet at a party. My brother and I, the only grandsons, and the minister, wearing a top hat straight out of one of pictures in old-fashioned Christmas cards, fell in behind them, and the men, some in bowler hats, stepped off the footpath and fell in behind us.

Only the men went to the graveyard; the women stayed in the house to make a big tea for them when they returned. We moved down the street in procession, everybody out of step, and because we were walking slowly, swaying sometimes from side to side, like the dying eel I once saw trying to swim up the grey stony bed of a river near Helen's Bay. Here and there a man on the footpath stopped, took off his hat, and as we passed the gable end of the Catholic Jamaica Street, a woman or two on their way to the grocer's shop, crossed themselves and waited until the coffin had passed before walking on. One of the horses pulling the hearse unloaded some balls of dung, and I had to step over them. The smell was awful, but I couldn't hold my nose because I would have looked disrespectful. I hoped that none of the horses would stop to flood the street like the milkman's horse.

From time to time, men took their turn to shoulder my Granda, until a man in a black top hat like the minister's and a long black coat and walking beside the hearse, nodded his head at my Daddy and Uncle John. We stopped while four men slid the coffin into the hearse. We walked on, following the hearse for a little while, and stopped again for the last time. Then everybody walked away, some to the carriages that had followed us and now would take us to Carnmoney Cemetery, the others I suppose, home, or back to work.

On the way to the graveyard I sat in one of the carriages facing my Granda Morrison and great-uncle Stanley. I had never been in a carriage before. Some funerals had motor-cars, but the war was still on and petrol was rationed. I had never been in a motor car either, but I liked the carriage. The leather seats smelled of olden days, and the carriage rocked gently even when it rolled over the peevers between the trammy lines. It was a long way from our house to the graveyard, and I wondered whether the horses ever got tired. All were black, with pure white fetlocks; their coats shone lovelier than the satin dresses in Robinson Cleaver's shop window, and the buckles of their harnesses gleamed. Even the black shafts shone. You could use the polished side of the carriage as a mirror to see if you had combed your hair straight.

Everything at a funeral is shiny, I thought, even Granda Morrison's face, even my face. Except Granda Porter's.

We rode up the rest of Alliance Avenue, the horses hooves' clipclop, clipclop, clipclop, like old bones hitting together, past big houses with three or more bedrooms and orchards in the back, the apple trees still bare from the Winter's breath, down Westland Road, where the horses wanted to gallop, for we could hear our driver shouting 'Whoa, whoa', past the Waterworks dam where you could sail toy yachts if you had a pass for admission, and on to the Antrim Road, where the houses were bigger than the ones on Alliance Avenue, and where the trammy lines ran all the way out to Glengormley, as far as you could ride for a ha'penny.

After a while, we passed Bellevue Park. The huge black chestnut and sycamore trees behind the hawthorn hedges were all trunks and arms, waiting for new fingers and fresh leaves. Elms stood like a row of upended brushes against the green-brown slopes. I felt an odd excitement seeing the high wide steps that led upward to the zoo. I tried to imagine what the animals were doing, at least those that were left. For the lions and tigers and elephants had been shot during the Blitz, for fear that a bomb falling nearby might burst open their cages and they would roam the streets killing people. Even so, it was a shame that they had to be killed.

Soon we reached the edge of the city, past the end of the trammy line, and at a steady trot the hearse and carriages turned on to a country road that led to the graveyard. I could see the Belfast Lough, and beyond it the distant low Holywood Hills. Behind us, on top of Carnmoney Mountain, a tall stone monument like a lonely sentry stood watch over the sleeping Lough.

The damp air smelt musty.

At the graveyard, my Granda was carried from the gates to where we would bury him. The men's feet soughed on the gravel path like the fall of small waves on the sea shore at Helen's Bay. The grave was the deepest hole in the ground I had ever seen, except for the crater left by the mine that exploded beside our school on the night of the third Blitz. But maybe it only looked deep because it was long and narrow. To one side lay a pile of soil and clay, and the fresh dank earth stung my nose. The two gravediggers lowered the coffin into the grave on ropes. I wondered if the ropes were buried as well, but the men pulled them out.

Everyone gathered around the grave, and the minister recited verses from the Bible about the Lord giving and the Lord taking away, and gathering up unto Himself the soul of our brother, by which he meant my Granda, and then he added the bit about 'earth to earth, and dust to dust, and ashes to ashes' and 'resurrection to eternal life', while a gravedigger dropped a handful of soil on the coffin. At the bottom of the grave the coffin looked small, and I remembered my solitary night visit to the wee bedroom, and my wonder that Granda should seem so small.

The thought I had reached for on that night now found words, or rather a word I had known for a long time but now felt. I now understood that death is what it does: it takes someone away, and leaves you 'remains'. A death in the family was different from deaths I had read in the paper. I had lost forever somebody I had really known, who mattered to me, who had filled my little blue and white bowl with sweet tea, and had listened to my stories, and tailored trousers, and every morning polished the chrome on his kitchen range, and every night swept up the ashes in his hearth before he went to bed. All *that* remained too, not in a grave but in my memory, and I could keep and carry these remains with me as long as I lived.

When the burial service ended, we stepped back while the grave diggers laid a purple pad on the coffin and began to shovel the mound of wet clay into the grave. The first shovelfuls thumped on the lid of the coffin, making a hollow sound as if the coffin was empty. I knew it wasn't, and yet I knew also it was, and for the first time since Granda died, I had a wee cry, quietly, just to myself.

Everybody drifted off among the graves, as if they were in no hurry to go home, reading the gravestones, and sometimes sighing 'Dear, dear' if it was a child's. A few graves were covered with withered wreaths; others with dead weeds and grass. Some were neat, covered with white pebbles or flint stones and fenced by low iron railings, painted black or silver, and spotted with rust where the paint had flaked. Here and there, at the foot of a headstone, sat a vase of sad-looking flowers covered by a long glass bowl, like the bottom of a huge test-tube, to protect the flowers, I suppose, from wind and rain. But the flowers had died anyway, bottled up in their own scent.

Bored with my wanderings, I joined my brother to poke among the gravel on the lanes between the graves, looking for pieces of flint stone. I pocketed a pair that sparked brightly, and was ready for the ride home, and the plates of sponge cake and the buns with the buttercream angel wings. The day had been long. Mammy would be waiting for us.

We went back to my Granda's grave before we left. It was now a long low mound, like a flower bed, covered with a thick coloured quilt of flowers and green ferns and leaves. Bending to read the little cards tied to the wreaths, I breathed in the scent of the flowers, fainter now than in the 'dead' room, but purer, like the armful of bluebells I gathered in spring for Mammy.

The smell of earth now, I noticed, had no sting.

Epilogue

That's the way it was, long ago, as it seemed to me when I was nearly twelve. I was too young to know that when Grandfather Porter died I had lost an irrecoverable past, a memory behind my own that would not be among the 'remains'. Most of it has passed into oblivion; for example, no one knows now how he remembered his parents, or how he, a shipyard worker, met and fell in love with my Grandma who grew up in a grand part of Belfast.

Mrs Hynes never again mentioned the smell of flowers in our house, even when they were roses from our small garden or bluebells from Carr's Glen. Had I known then what I know now about logic, I might have been able to persuade her that her unwitting premonition had no causal effect. It probably wouldn't have been helpful anyway. Irish lore is full of beliefs about banshee wails predicting sorrows and premonitions having causal powers, and reason is usually powerless against superstitions.

Most of the people I knew then are gone now, some long dead, among them Joe, the insurance man, and Mrs Hynes. My mother wrote to me about her death, for I was living in Canada, and she spoke warmly of their long friendship, especially of Vi's comfort during and after her sorrow. She added, with sadness, that she would miss her *craic*, and Joe's. In their long friendship, most of their tears flowed from laughter.

To this day, when I smell the funereal odour of lilies, against all reason I catch my breath while the shadow of a residual superstition flits across my mind.

Chapter 16
THE LAUNCH

ON THE morning of the first day of my working life, I checked my appearance in the wardrobe mirror: lightly oiled hair parted almost straight along the side of the head, no blear in the eyes, no wrinkles in the white shirt, no spots on its starched collar, tie properly knotted, shoes gleaming, hems of the trouser legs even across my kneecaps, and lastly, socks properly at full mast. At another time, in the past, I would have admired myself. But not on that morning, the Second of June, 1947.

Fresh out of school as a herring tossed off a Friday morning trawler on to a fishmonger's cart (but with better prospects), I had a job at the Main Offices of the 'Island', the soubriquet for the Belfast shipyard. My father and three uncles were Islandmen, a breed apart among industrial workers in the city. Now I was too, a tyro, to be sure, but of the breed, my name on the books.

I was immaculate, but not happy with what I saw in the mirror.

Islandmen do not wear short trousers and knee-length socks held up with elastic bands.

It was bad enough that my nerves nipped at my kidneys, but that dressed in short trousers I would tramp alongside Islandmen across the Queen's Bridge toward the Yard stung my soul like a recent shame.

The Seventh Standard schoolmaster, Nipper Quinn, should have paid heed to my arms flailing the air like a bather drowning, to my frantic irruptions into his gabble on Euclid's theorems: 'Sir! Sir!' Unable to bear the pain in my bladder any longer, I had dashed for the classroom door. Behind the last row of desks I doubled up, as if hit below the belt. The flood spilled toward the desk where sat a girl I fancied. Later, wet and skulking in a lavatory cubicle, I overheard my school mates having a laugh, not an entirely unsympathetic one, about wee Willie's weak bladder. The shame had stalked the rest of my school days, and on the day I left I thought I could outrun it. Now, it came out from the mirror to mock my sartorial state. Islandman. Island*man*? Yer coddin' yerself, wee Willie.

My metamorphosis from schoolboy to worker had been abrupt, and without ceremony. At roll call on the morning of my birthday, Nipper announced to all the world as he addressed me in particular, 'I see you're fourteen now, Morrison. You'll be leaving us this afternoon.' The class murmured and stirred, and some boys cheered. Nipper barked for silence, and continued by name to herd his flock. Later in the day, he handed me a school leaving card which I would need for employers. No valediction urged me to follow dreams and ideals. Nipper merely wished me well, and the class hooted its farewell.

Let out before school was dismissed, I didn't wait around to be mobbed by envious mates, but raced up Ardoyne Loney, my old leather schoolbag swinging from the crook of my left arm for the last time. At home, I flung it behind the front door, as I always did, and with it the burden of school, and of being a schoolboy.

I

I had known for a while that I was bound for an apprenticeship at the Island, or the Yard, as it was sometimes called. Until it began, on my sixteenth birthday, I would run messages at the Main Offices. Still, the suddenness of my metamorphosis caught my mother unprepared.

'So ye're done with school nigh, son,' she said, when I clattered into the kitchen.

'Yis,' I answered. In my state of mind, the monosyllable was an understatement, but I was always shy with words for feelings, except when I was angry. The afternoon was warm. I was hot, sweating, and out of breath after my run from school, but my mind had already been a step ahead of her.

'I'll be needin' longs,' I said.

'Ye'll have t'wait, Will, until I have enough money in th' Co-op club,' she said. 'For the time bein' ye'll have t'put up wi' short trousers.'

She might as well have spilled cold water down the neck of my jersey.

My father, a labourer, earned a meagre wage, and I knew that my mother didn't see all of it, for though he didn't drink, he smoked like a regiment of troopers, and bet on horses. My mother used the Belfast Cooperative club as a kind of saving account for things she needed besides food and rent. I grumbled about having to go to work looking like a schoolboy, but bent to her will. Maybe the 'time being' would not be long.

It was an age when a boy's sartorial transition from short to long trousers was a social rite of passage that usually occurred close to his fourteenth birthday. In his new pair of grey flannels he would present himself shyly to his aunts and uncles, and they would say:

'Well, here he is. You're a right man nigh. Here's silver for yer pocket. Bring ye good luck.'

If he had a clan of aunts and uncles, he made a small fortune. An uncle would ask, and answer his own question,

'D'ye know how t'keep creases in yer trousers straight and sharp? Line up th' seams an' use a damp cloth when ye irn th'legs.'
Soon he would be arguing the toss with him about football, or politics. Man to man. Well, to boy-man. His life so far would be summed up succinctly by a neighbour he and his mother would meet on the street where he grew up:

'My, Missus Marisen, hasn't your Will grow'd.'
And addressing him, she would take a step back, fold her arms tightly under her bosom, tip her head to one side, and size him up:

'God love ye. Sure I mind ye when ye run about wi' a dummy tit in yer gob, an' th' snatters trippin' ye. An' nigh yer in longs, a right wee man. Oh aye. Ye'll be havin' the girls after ye soon.'
His ears would burn, and he would silently hope she is right, and, seeing his discomfort she would become coy:

'Maybe, have ye clicked already?'
And he would protest, and wish it was true.

To crown his new sense of himself, he would chuck his peakfrayed skull cap into the dustbin and don a duncher, and maybe learn to swagger. And he would discover soon, that experience would be a harsher master than any who had caned him.

So far, no silver jingled in my pockets except what I had earned, my trousers needed no crease, and no girls were chasing me, even though I wore a duncher. And the girl I fancied, I hadn't clicked yet, for would she walk the Horseshoe Road with an Islandman launched into the world half-naked below the waist? Or would she choose someone who worked in Wolfhill Spinning Mill or Ewart's flax mill, a real 'wee man' from head to toe?

Before I left school, I used to watch with envy these 'wee men' only months older than myself clattering along our street in heavy boots, dunchers and overalls. Some of my school mates were going into the mill. They would earn good money, better than office boys or messengers. 'No, son,' my father said, when I hinted at working there. He had worked in a bleach mill, before he took a job at the shipyard. 'A trade's what ye want. The big money'll come in time. An' ye cin take yer trade anywhere.' I deferred to him, assured within myself that in spite of my slight build I was as tough as any mill boy. But I prayed to whichever deity governed chance, that on my way to and from work in short trousers, I would never meet a former classmate in his overalls and big boots.

My mother's 'time being' began to stretch into weeks. Each morning, smartly dressed but for the unsightly bulge of coat pocket where my 'piece' – sandwiches wrapped in brown paper – was rammed, duncher at the Islandman angle on my head, I walked at a steady pace (for you can't swagger in short trousers) from Castle Junction, down High Street, by the Albert Clock, and over the Queen's Bridge towards the Queen's Road. Sometimes, a wind from the Lough played about my knees.

My boss, Sergeant Hermann, the Hall Porter, a bantam-size member of the Corps of Commissionaires, was the doorkeeper at the grand entrance to the Main Offices on Queen's Road. With its revolving door and marble floors, it resembled the foyer of a posh hotel and was used only by Harland & Wolff directors, and distinguished visitors. The battalion of clerks, accountants, typists and draughtsmen entered the Main Offices by side and back doors.

The Sergeant attended to the comings and goings of the Chairman, Sir Frederick Rebbeck and the Company Directors, phoning for cars, opening doors, brushing overcoats, and wiping shoes coated with the dust of their danders among slipways, under gantries, through sheds, or on board ships. He had three messengers under his command. The office staff, with a touch of prurience, nicknamed us 'The Sergeant's boys'.

As the most junior of the Hall Porter's three boys, twice each day I scurried through the warren of offices – Drawing Office, Accounts, Purchasing, Receiving, and Cashier – to collect, distribute, and deposit mail and memos. Now and again a clerk and or typist taunted me with mock admiration of my naked knees and neat bum. One typist hiked her skirt: 'Like that, Willie?' she said, presenting me with a slender length of leg. Her colleagues cackled, I blushed, and had enough sense to grin, for now I had a boast to make before my mates. But one incident troubled me, and of it I dared not boast. A clerk dropped a pencil beside me, and as I bent to pick it up, I heard low laughter, and turned. Behind me, and almost against me, a fellow had dropped into a crouch, like a rugby player waiting for a loose ball to be tossed back. Recognising the gesture, and not grinning this time in response, but on the edge of tears, I cursed my naïveté, and my mother's penury.

The teasing faded within days, but it lingered in my mind. Still, I drew some self-esteem from the nature of my job. In the Hall Porter's office, we spent most of the day waiting; waiting to deliver a message, usually a telegram, from the switchboard operator across the hall, to Sir Frederick or one of the others Directors; waiting to jump to a passing Director's summons, 'Boy!', which in my case, I thought ruefully, seemed appropriate rather than offensive; waiting for the arrival of Sir Frederick or a Director or a distinguished visitor, at which the Sergeant would bark 'Up, boys!' and two of us would rush out of the office to hold open the main doors to the Board's wing of the building. 'Morning, sir,' the Sergeant would sing out, and if it was Sir Frederick, he would answer, 'Morning, Sergeant,' and nod to us as he passed between the open doors on his way upstairs, where the company Directors had their offices.

'Upstairs'. To me the word evoked another world, a hushed, reverent world redolent of wealth. Here the offices were not featureless rooms with worn floorboards and faded linoleum and walls that appeared as bored as the figures that bent over desks; they were an elegant, plush domain of deep carpets, of panelled walls bearing oil paintings and photographs of ships, of superbly crafted model ships in glass cases, of period furniture and massive oak desks, and immaculate washrooms. It was a world I had known only in fiction and in films. Each time I entered it, I inhaled with the scented wax of furniture polish the intoxicating odour of wealth and power. The men who occupied this domain spoke in educated English accents, smoked cigars and the best of cigarettes, drank the finest whiskeys and sherries and port wines.

The first time I took a telegram to Sir Frederick, my heart raced and I suddenly needed to pee, a sign of an atavistic anxiety about entering the presence of the rich and powerful. How I should behave? Be as inconspicuous as possible, my intuition told me. Neither slouch nor fart, my breeding warned me.

I raced up the stairs, composed myself outside Sir Frederick's office, knocked timidly on the door, and then boldly. A loud, deep, educated voice called, 'Come in,' and I entered a fug of cigar smoke. As I crossed the expanse between the door and Sir Frederick's desk, I had the odd feeling that I was walking on air, but it was only the sensation of walking on deep carpet. Sir Frederick, tall and stout, a cigar between two fingers of his right hand, took the telegram and read it. He thanked me quietly and dismissed me, and I glided out of his presence, like a ship on a calm sea steaming through a light fog. Despite my fears, I had not wet myself.

At home, my self-importance grew, at least in the presence of my brother and sisters, when I reported from time to time at the dinner table my doings among the rich and powerful:

'You should see Sir Frederick's office, no oilcloth on th' floor, carpet you sink into.'

And everyone at the table would glance at the thin mats on our oilcloth covered floorboards.

'I collected wine glasses th' day in th' Board Room. You should have seen th' size of the butts Directors leave in ash trays. Didn't have the nerve to pocket them. You could've rolled them, Daddy, into full cigarettes.'

I would be half-serious, and my siblings would giggle, and my mother would tut-tut, and my father would frown, 'Don't you dare'.

'Had to go to th' Directors' dining room. Like th' Grand Central Hotel. And the waiter wears tails. Like, you know, the Marx brothers. Or Charlie Chaplin.'

Over time, these avid reportings, the inevitable comparisons with our world of kitchen houses and plain fare, and my cheap self-aggrandisement at the expense of the family, must have begun to irritate my mother. One evening at dinnertime, in tones of reverence and awe, I described the Directors' lavatory and, as usual drew a comparison with our own:

'I wis upstairs t'day, an' th' door to th' Directors' lavatory wis slightly open. I went in. You should'av seen it. Beautiful. White tiled walls, marble floor, marble wash basins wi' gold taps, an' a pure white toilet bowl. An' it smelled, not of Lifebuoy soap like ours does, but like a perfume shop. It smelled more than clean. I wanted to pee into th' toilet jus' for th' luxurious thrill of it.'

'An' why didn't ye?' my mother interrupted.

'I could'of,' I said, ''cause I wis so nervous of bein' caught prying in a privy, an' I could have done it in full spate.'

Everyone laughed at that, and I went on:

'Ye know, th' rich don't wipe their bums wi' squares of newspaper like we do, but with soft, soft tissue paper, an' they don't sit on a wooden toilet seat like our toilet has, but on soft white ones – or so it seemed – an' their lavatory chains have fancy gold handles.'

My mother had had enough of my fascination with the privileges of the rich:

'Son,' she said, her voice firm as if she was about to lay down the law, 'they might sit on soft seats, an' wipe wi' soft paper, and pull a gold chain, but they still have to shite like the rest of us.'

Our mother's coining of the truism convulsed us with laughter. But I detected in it too, her sensitivity to our mean circumstances which I, with my admiring descriptions of privilege, served only to underscore, and which she, with the little she had, had tried to overcome.

Still, my tenuous familiarity with the world 'Upstairs' sustained me at those moments when, on comparing myself with the 'wee men' in the flax and spinning mills in our neighbourhood, I would become despondent. Whatever the import of the telegrams and other messages I carried, they made me feel important, however illusory that feeling was, by the mere fact that I was a link in a chain of events, like a telegram boy in the films I had seen, who has no lines to deliver but whose fleeting presence is a cue to a shift in the action.

One late September afternoon, close to the end of the working day, when my mates and the Sergeant had gone home and I, as the most junior boy had to stay until the official time for leaving work, a switchboard operator at Reception across the hall vigorously summoned me: 'Take this to Sir Frederick as fast as you can. Run.' She handed me a small envelope containing a telegram. I took the stairs two at a time, as if the devil was at my back. On the following morning I learned that late in the afternoon of the previous day the engines of the *Reina del Pacifico*, a liner on sea trials after a reconversion from troopship to passenger service at the Yard, had exploded, killing instantly twenty-eight men and horribly burning and scalding twice that number, all of them Islandmen. The telegram conveyed the news to Sir Frederick.

II

Summer passed its zenith, and I was still not in longs. I knew that this state of affairs couldn't last much longer, for surely by now my mother had enough money in the Co-op club to buy me flannels. 'Not just yit,' she would say, when I raised the matter. 'Just be patient a wee bit longer.' I needed a reason to force the issue. One evening, a newspaper headline laid it in my lap.

The Belfast Telegraph announced that Princess Margaret, the seventeen-year-old daughter of King George VI was coming to Belfast to launch a ship. I knew then that my weeks of bare-kneed angst were about to come to an end. The postwar 1940s were among the busiest in the Yard's history. The slipways were full, orders for all kinds of vessels were being launched: tugs, whale-factory ships, oil tankers, cargo ships, cargo-passenger ships, and even a paddle-steamer named *Waverley*. But the pride of the Yard were the magnificent passenger ships. 'Boats', Islandmen called them.

The world had heard of the *Titanic*, the *Olympic* and *Britannic*, because of their fates, but the Yard had built many great liners. Their exotic names read like a geography of the world, *Arlanza, Austurius, Andes, Minnekahda, Regina Pittsburg, Laurentia, Narkunda, Mooltan, Maloja, Doric, Statendam, Reina del Pacifico, Minnewaska, Minnetonka, Rajputana, Rawalpindi*. The Castle Line had its own Belfast roll of honour: *Arundel Castle, Warwick Castle, Llangibby Castle, Dunbar Castle, Winchester Castle, Stirling Castle, Athlone Castle, Dunottar Castle, Dunvegan Castle, Capetown Castle*.

When one made the newspaper headlines or was bruited on the wireless – some were sunk by U-boats during the Second World War – somewhere in Belfast an Islandman would be saying at his dinner in a kitchen or to friends and strangers in a pub, 'I worked on her, an' I mind th' day she went down the slips.'

Indeed. And, although I didn't work on the *Pretoria Castle* – my own naming of maritime names was still to come – I mind the day she went down the slipway in the Musgrave Yard, launched by remote control from Pretoria, South Africa by Sybella Smuts, the wife of the South African Premier. It was an historic launching, a first in the world of shipbuilding: an electric impulse sent along a radio link, which the BBC had helped to set up, would release the trigger holding the ship.

The launch took place during a lunch hour, as it usually did to allow workers to attend. By the time I arrived breathless at the slipway, for I had run from the Main Offices to the Musgrave Yard, a garrulous crowd of workers and spectators from the city was already swirling around the launch platform and the bow of the ship. The slipway echoed with the thuds of sledgehammers as shipwrights and their helpers knocked away the keel blocks and wedged into place the cradles on which the hull would rest as it slid into the water. Occasional blasts of tugboat horns punctured the echoes. A blend of ozone from oily sea water and the odour of tallow and tobacco filled the air. I could taste its pungency, and my nostrils stung. Overhead, the arms of towering gantry cranes at rest crisscrossed the blue August sky.

The colossal gleaming black and buff hull of the *Pretoria Castle*, hundreds of feet in length, and now stripped of the tiers of scaffolding that had risen around it in the weeks it had been raised rib by rib and plate by plate from its broad keel, lay like an elegant leviathan stranded on a narrow stretch of beach. Beneath it, Lilliputian shipwrights and their helpers moved among the keel blocks and tall timbers on which it rested. The magnificence of the work, that such a mass of steel plate could be shaped into a thing of beauty, with graceful sweeping curves from bow to stern and abeam, filled me with the awe one usually reserves for a breathtaking scene of natural beauty.

Along the bulwarks of the bow, which soared and fanned out perhaps a hundred feet or more above me, I could see, in silhouette against the sky the bobbing dunchers of the men who remained on board for the launching. At the peak of the bow, a row of pale faces peered down on the crowd.

At launching hour's approach, the metronomic thud of sledgehammers died away. The air, it seemed, suddenly stilled. The crowd, now dense, had ceased eddying around the launching platform, and stood still, looking up as if in expectation of some Second Coming. Men checked their pocket-watches and called out the time. Wreaths of pipe and cigarette smoke hung over the crowd like incense above a congregation.

Then, as if bidden by an unseen hand, the murmurs and chattering of the multitude of voices faded into a churchly quiet. The tugboats at the mouth of the Musgrave Channel became mute.

Out of the silence a light, clear, female voice from six thousand miles away floated eerily above the crackle of the airwaves: 'I name this ship the *Pretoria Castle*. May God bless her and all that sail in her.' A bottle crashed faintly against steel, and a shower of champagne splashed the ship's bow and cascaded to the ground below.

Nothing happened. The crowd, still silent, waited. Then, almost imperceptibly, the hull began to move, as though it was in no hurry to reach the sea. A murmur stirred among the crowd, it grew in volume, and as the gap widened between the ship's bow and the launch platform, it swelled into a cheer like a mighty organ in full vent. Tugboats picked up on the crowd's roar and broke into a raucous din of blaring horns and ululating wail of sirens that surely must have awakened the gods dormant on Cave

Hill since the days of St Patrick. Men waved their dunchers toward the ship, men on the deck waved down to their brother workers. The cheering continued as the hull picked up momentum. The launch had begun.

The hull, gliding on a bed of tallow, picked up speed. Thick steel cables, stretching from the bulwarks to drag weights of huge piles of chain on the ground, tightened and strained to check its accelerating slide into the sea. One cable, unable to bear the tension, snapped and whirled into the air, a lethal lariat whose trajectory could cut a man in two. A roar burst from the crowd, and though in no danger, men instinctively moved back from the slipway.

In less than a minute since it had begun to move, the stern of the hull smoothly entered the water. Waves rolled up each side of the slipway as if to draw the vessel fully in the sea's embrace. It rocked a few times, then settled on an even keel, and the cradles on which it had rested during its slide floated free. Tugboats closed in to take up the hawsers that fell from the main deck, and began to tow the hull gently to its new berth.

The baptism was over. I had been unprepared for the emotional power of the ritual, the priestly naming of the ship, its graceful quiet movement at a woman's bidding, into its natural element, the sea. What its builders dreamed, it had become, and they were proud of their work. The *Pretoria Castle* was ready now to be fitted out for service upon the oceans of the world.

Men drifted back to their work at other slipways, in shops and sheds, and spectators dandered towards the tram stops on Queen's Road. Behind them, and between neighbouring slipways where other ships were in the making, lay the enormous empty berth open to the sky and as silent and desolate as the nave of a great ruined cathedral. But it would not be so for long; within a few days the melancholy quiet would be swallowed up in the thunder of riveters laying down another keel, the embryo of a new vessel, and many months later the rite would be repeated.

On a slipway nearby the skeletal ribs of the *Edinburgh Castle* pointed to the sky. In two months Princess Margaret would bless it and send it into the sea.

The morning after the newspaper announcement about the royal visit, the Sergeant informed us that the Princess would be coming to the Main Offices for a reception after the launch. 'You will be on the doors,' he said.

It was time to confront my mother, to beg, borrow or steal the money for the trousers, if she couldn't afford them now.

'The other boy wears longs,' I said. 'I would feel half-dressed,' I whinged. 'The Princess would see a mere boy opening the door for her. She would notice my knees, their trembling, and maybe she would giggle, and I would be ashamed. Worse, sacked,' I moaned.

My mother listened in amusement to my foolish arguments, whose truth, except for the first one, I too doubted as I uttered them, but hoped by raising a laugh from my brother and sisters, I would convince my mother how ridiculous was my situation.

'Ye'll have yer flannel trousers in time for Princess Margaret's visit,' she promised.

She kept her promise, and I stepped into manhood, in a manner of speaking.

About a month before the royal visit, with her Co-op book in her purse, she took me downtown. A tailor measured my waist, and then knelt in front of me and ran his tape the length of my leg.

'Which side do you dress to?' he asked.
I didn't understand the question, having never bought longs, and thought it had something to do with whether I was right or left-handed.

'Well, I'm left-handed,' I replied.
The tailor looked up at my mother, who rolled her eyes, and I knew I had said something stupid. He pulled the trousers slightly in the area of my groin.

'Well, you have to be comfortable around here,' he said.
I caught on immediately, and coloured.

'Oh,' I said, and felt fearful that he might have thought that I had taken his question as a sarcasm about boy's penchant for having a hole in one trouser pocket.

The transition from short trousers, which seemed to take care of the male member without fuss about where it should be comfortably housed, to long trousers, which made an issue out of it, proved to be more complicated and significant than I had anticipated.

A week later I appeared at the Hall Porter's office in new grey flannels with creases as sharp as a hatchet blade. The Sergeant gave me an approving wink and smile. I could see that he was amused. For the first time I looked forward to the mail run. If I was paid a ten-bob for every time a clerk or typist said, 'We'll miss yer knees, Willie', I could have bought pinstripes instead of flannels. From time to time I glanced at the left side of my groin, but it looked no different than the right.

The Sergeant rehearsed us on our duty. He was back on the parade ground in Victoria Barracks. At his command we leapt and scurried to our positions at the doors. Opened them on cue – the nod of his head – and closed them on cue.

'You will remain at the doors throughout the reception, no matter how long you have to stand there, until I tell you to return to your bench. Keep your hands out of pockets at all times.'

'And fingers out of noses,' I added under my breath. The longs were having their effect on my character.

'You will stand up straight; you will not slouch,' he went on.
I pulled my shoulders back, my stomach in, and immediately discovered how important the tailor's question proved to be.

'You will have your hair combed, your tie properly knotted, blazer properly buttoned, flannels properly creased, and shoes with a shine you can see your face in,' he concluded.

He paused, perhaps to let us bark 'Yes, sir!' like recruits halfway through their basic training, but we only nodded slightly to let him know we had heard him and would obey him, and he returned from the barrack square to the Main Office hall.

One question I thought deserved airing, but I let it pass; it was not a manly question. But what should we do if, while we were on duty at the door, we were suddenly overtaken by an urgent need to go to the lavatory? It would not be manly to have to abandon one's post at the moment the

Princess needed us. The memory of my humiliation in Nipper Quinn's class flickered briefly across my mind. All I could do was hope that I would not fail.

On a dull mid-October day, the Princess, in a dusky pink coat with a dark fur-lined collar, arrived at the Main Offices with her entourage. The party dithered for a moment in the hall. The Sergeant, in regimental dress, nodded to us, and we swung open the doors to the Board Room. As if that had been her cue, the Princess, with Sir Frederick at her side, moved toward us.

The Sergeant bowed slightly, like a toy soldier about to tilt forward, and when the Princess reached the door, I lowered my head, as if in prayer. As she passed by me I looked up, and smiled. She glanced my way and smiled, not a full smile, but slight. But it was the glance, the luminous glance of the dark royal eyes that imprinted itself indelibly on my mind. It lasted but an instant, like the click of a camera. My heart raced as if I had hurled myself from the starting blocks in a sprint, and the real world faded to a shadow, like the darkened backdrop of a moonlit stage.

She was three years older than me, she was unattainable, and I was wearing longs and no longer believed in fairy tales. But while I waited for the royal party to return from their sherry and gin, the imaginings of my naïve heart pulverised my unbelief. Felled by a glance, I had fallen for the Princess.

I was already half in love with a girl who, on Sunday mornings, sat on the other side of the gallery in church, and who surely must have noticed that I was now in longs. I hadn't declared myself, content for the moment with fancying I was in love, and so I was free to shift my allegiance to another.

When the entourage returned from the reception, I tried to catch the eye of the Princess as she passed, that I might be emboldened by a knowing smile and nod of the head to convey my undying fealty, but the stout Sir Frederick by her side shielded her from my view, and I watched her walk away, step by lovely step, out of my life forever.

For a while I carried the image of the lovely eyes and slender form before me as a knight-at-arms bears his lady's image on his shield. I was no longer wee Willie the forlorn, with the weak bladder and bare knees. A royal glance had transformed me, even though I knew that fairy tales end in a lie. My fealty proved to be ephemeral, and soon I replaced her image with another, a more attainable girl, who, her emissary had informed me, fancied me, and whom, in my new flanneled self-assurance, I might just click. My amorous prospects had improved.

I wrote short letters to her, for my new self-assurance was still not assured enough for me to present myself to her in person. I carried them in my pocket for a few days, and then shredded them into a wastepaper basket. Fealty, in this case, wasn't necessary. A month or two later, without her ever finding out how I adored her, on paper at least, she chucked me for a fellow with a motorcycle, who probably worked at a mill. I did not even have a bicycle, and so, once again in the stakes of love I was out of my league, despite the length of my trousers.

My heart did not break, for neither clicking nor being clicked truly mattered to me. I had slipped the last sartorial bond of boyhood, and fully dressed for manhood – comfortably on the left side – I had left behind forever the secure berth of school for the unknown and complicated world of work and love. No invocation of blessing, no champagne, no cheering crowd, no fanfare of horns or wailing of sirens, no girl by my side, to welcome me into my new estate. I did not care.

Each day at 5.30pm I left the Main Offices to walk the mile or so to the city's centre. My navy Burberry belted comfortably around me, my duncher firmly on my head, one hand in the pocket of my overcoat, one arm swinging confidently, and my flannel trousers caressing my shins with each step, I strode along the Queen's Road, past the Co. Down Railway Station, by the coal sheds on the quay side, and over the Queen's Bridge. I walked to the rhythm of boots tramping, scraping, echoing all around me, their rhythms and mine submerging into one sonorous swell of Islandmen slogging home from work, and I felt the ineffable joy of being in full communion with that great company.

Epilogue

I could not foresee, in that summer of '47 that my years as an Islandman would be brief (seven in all), that the working life I had imagined for myself when I pulled on my first pair of longs would undergo sea changes which would take me to another continent. Nor did any Islandman, I suppose, who on the Queen's Bridge passed or walked alongside a boy in short trousers, foresee that one day only the ghostly echoes of memories would stir when the wind blew across the deserted Yard's barren landscape.

Chapter 17

WEALTH AND WELSH RABBIT

THE COLD deceptive December drizzle that had fallen all afternoon on the city now sifted through the darkness as I walked the mile or so from the shipyard to the city's centre. Usually on such a night I would be anxious to get home before the damp seeped through my sodden overcoat to chill my bones. But not tonight, for it was Christmas Eve, and I would not be home for tea. Silver coins in my trouser pocket sang to the steady measure of my footfalls, and from time to time I whistled to the rhythms of my happiness. My only care was the choice of the right restaurant to patronise with my pocketful of wealth.

It was my mother's idea. On an overcast Christmas Eve morning, she came to the front door to see me off to work.

'Treat yourself on th' way home th' night. Have your tea downtown,' she said.

'Ye mean, not come straight home?' I asked.

Since I had started work as a message boy in the Hall Porter's office at the shipyard's Main Offices seven months earlier, I had always come home for tea. I was only fourteen years of age, too young to drink stout in pubs, and not rich enough to buy my dinner when I fancied.

My wits took longer to waken than my limbs.

'Ye mean, have me tea at a chip shop?'

Some fish and chip shops had a bit of class. They served tea and bread with the fish suppers, and you ate with a knife and fork rather than with you fingers, from a plate set on a linen tablecloth.

'Don't be daft,' she said. 'Go t' a restaurant downtown.'

183

I had been in cafés for sandwiches and cakes, but never had a dinner in a real restaurant.

'What one will I go to?' I asked.

'For God's sake, Will, have a titter of wit. One on High Street, or Ann Street.'

'But they're dear. More than fish an' chip shops.'

'You'll have your Christmas boxes, won't ye?'

Now I was wide awake. Unknown to herself, she had swatted a worry that had been flitting about in my head for the past few days.

Every Friday night I gave my mother my unopened pay packet. When my mates boasted that they kept theirs, I said nothing, for they would banter me for being under my mother's thumb. Anyway, my wages were so meagre, just a few shillings, that little was left after she set aside my tram fare to the shipyard and gave me pocket money, the amount of which we had settled by agreement. The first pay packet I had given her she handed back to me.

'You're a working man nigh. Take Herbie to th' pictures,' she had said.

Herbie, my chum since I was seven years old, lived next door. We were a month apart in age, and I had been the first to go to work. We took a tram to the Capitol Cinema near Fortwilliam Park in the swanky part of the Antrim Road, to see King Kong. Unlike the flea pits where we spent Saturday afternoons, the Capitol was plush. I bought tickets for balcony seats, which cost more than the pit, and during the show, I treated us both to ice cream and chocolate bars bought from an usherette, who paraded unerringly up and down the ebony steps of the balcony with her tray of treats suspended from her neck like a halter. We walked home, and although I hadn't a penny left in my pocket for tram fares, I had tasted the sweetness of affluence.

Christmas boxes weren't bonuses; they came from department heads and clerks in the offices where you worked. Two bob here, half-a-crown there, maybe a ten-shilling note. They could mount to a tidy sum, and I had great expectations of nothing less than a small fortune, because I was a messenger for four of Harland and Wolff's Directors. Warnings from older more experienced messengers in other offices that the Directors were

Scrooges shook but didn't demolish my optimism. But I had worried that this prospective wealth wouldn't be mine to keep. On my way to the tram which would take me to work, I parsed my mother's question.

She didn't say, 'You'll get Christmas boxes'. She said, 'You'll HAVE YOUR Christmas boxes'. 'Have' means 'to possess'. 'Your' is in the possessive case.

Satisfied that her meaning was clear, I whistled down the street at full throttle into the grey light of early morning, no doubt confusing the sparrows nesting in the eaves of the half-awake tone-deaf houses.

The drizzle showed no signs of easing as I rounded the corner of Ann Street into Victoria Street. I glanced up at the Albert Clock. Ten minutes to six. The clock, a memorial to the dead consort of a dead queen, had four faces so that it could be read from whatever direction one approached it. It towered about a hundred feet into the air, at a tilt because it was built on unstable ground close to a bank of the River Lagan. The falling drizzle seemed like a sifting of salt as it drifted past its bright yellow face, too fine for snow. I slowed my pace for I was in no hurry now.

At the foot of the tower, I turned into High Street, passed the darkened St George's Church of Ireland, and stopped at the window of the first restaurant I came upon.

Condensation covered the window so that I couldn't see whether the place was clean and inviting. Unsure of myself, I dallied for a few minutes. Pedestrians hurried by, some under umbrellas, others hunched against the glimmering pinpoints floating downward through the lamp light. My overcoat glistened as though showered with dew, and my feet were beginning to draw the cold damp from the wet pavement.

I stepped into the restaurant's narrow vestibule. A 'BILL of FARE' was displayed on a side window, and I skimmed it, checking the prices. The cheapest dinner was more than a double fish and chip supper. I dithered. I remembered a café on York Street, not far from where I stood.

My mother had taken my brother, sisters and me to it after a shopping spree for new socks and shoes. After we settled ourselves in a booth, she picked up the menu propped in a glass holder on the blue and white chequered tablecloth. We watched her closely, as if she was a character in a film about to read a crucial letter. Seconds passed like the weeks before Christmas.

She looked at each of us, her face blank. We stared, our mouths half-open.

'To hell with poverty!' she cried, and struck the table with her fist. 'We'll have bread an' tea with our chips. And two fish between ye.'
And we laughed at her outrageous defiance of our lot, and I loved the glister in her blue eyes. For a moment, even if only in imagination, we were rich.

I fingered the coins resting in my trouser pocket, and glanced up at the Albert. It beamed indifferently into the wet darkness. 'To hell with poverty,' I said to myself, consciously echoing my mother, and pushed open the restaurant door.

An odour of damp coats and cigarettes and food and the chatter of diners amid the clatter of dishes and cutlery drew me into the humid warmth. The restaurant was neither large nor spacious, its tables quite close together. The decor was not quite what I had expected. I had expected decorum; dark mahogany wainscot, crystal chandeliers radiating sparkling light, an intricately designed ceiling, and a *maitre d'* in black and white, with large beribboned leatherback menus clutched to his chest, like a Plymouth brother nursing his Bible at a street corner. Instead, colourful paper decorations like overstretched accordions looped across the white ceiling and along sea-green walls like holiday bunting; red paper bells dangled from overhead lights and lazily turned in the smoky air.

A waitress cheerfully pointed me to a table at which a man and a woman were sitting. I shook myself free of my sodden overcoat, and of my overblown expectations. After all, this was Belfast, not the London, Paris or New York that I had seen in films. I hung the coat on a crowded damp rack near the restaurant's entrance, and stood hesitantly at the table to which I had been directed.

Sensing my indecision the waitress came to my aid, muttered something about the restaurant being crowded out on Christmas Eve, and apologised to the couple already seated. I thought I should apologise too, but didn't. The couple nodded. I returned a shy smile, and sat down in a chair close to a wall.

The gay decorations gave the place a festive air. At crowded tables patrons talked with animation. Here and there a column of cigarette smoke spiralled toward a paper bell and spun itself around it. Everyone seemed to be with someone, some had brightly wrapped parcels and bulging shopping bags stowed at their feet, With a twinge of unease I realised that I was the youngest patron there. But the gaiety of the place – it was Christmas Eve, after all – banished my anxiety, and I felt at ease with my choice, and happy.

Three waitresses in black dresses, white aprons, and white cotton tiaras bustled to and fro between the kitchen and the restaurant. I marvelled as each, with a laden tray held aloft on her hand, feinted unerringly with a swing of her hips between the closely placed tables. But none looked as classy as Andre, the chef-cum-*maitre d'* at the Directors' dining hall in the shipyard, sailing down the hallway of the Main Offices with a tray of sherry and whiskey glasses.

To me, Andre was the epitome of elegant waiterhood. A tall Frenchman, black-haired, dark eyed, with a purplish closely shaved chin, he spoke English with a resonant accent. At 10.30 every weekday morning I picked up at his kitchen a can of hot tea in a brown paper bag for my boss, the Hall Porter. Drinking tea or coffee during working hours was not permitted anywhere in the shipyard, and violators could be punished by either a suspension of pay or the sack. Andre, in his chef's attire, white coat and apron, tall white hat on his head, would hand me the bag and caution me to be alert for any Director who might be wandering the long hallway by which I returned to the Hall Porter's office. For luncheon at the dining hall he would change into the formal wear of a *maitre d'*: black hammer-tails, black trousers with a shining black stripe down the side of each leg, white shirt, black bow tie, and his black hair slicked back from his balding forehead.

On certain afternoons he served sherry and whiskey at receptions in the Directors' Board Room. We would catch him passing by our office, a tray of glasses balanced on one hand, his coat-tails flapping against the back of his legs as if propelling him along, and one of us would dash to open the door to the Board Room for him. He would sail elegantly through the doorway, his back straight, his head erect, a waft of fragrance in his wake. I was never sure whether the fragrance came from his hair oil or freshly-shaved purple chin or from his clothing. 'Perfume,' my mates said, and rolled their eyes. After these receptions, we would gather the empty glasses redolent of sherry and whiskey, inhale them, and, more rarely and daringly, sip at a dreg, before carrying them back to Andre's kitchen.

For all his elegance, Andre was not aloof; he traded banter with us, we addressed him by his first name. I believed, mistakenly because of my familiarity with him, that I would never be intimidated by any waiter or nor even by a *maitre d'*.

A waitress handed me the BILL of FARE, and left. As I had noted outside the restaurant, the meals were pricey for my pay packet, but tonight I was a man of other means. I ran my fingers through the coins in my trouser pocket.

A few moments later, the waitress returned.

'What will you have, sir?'

Her voice was pleasant. I blushed, as if I had been caught reading a spicy article in the *News of the World*. I hastily skimmed the menu again: Roast Lamb, Turkey, Chicken, Steak, Mixed Grill, Plaice, Welsh Rabbit, Steak and Kidney Pie, Shepherd's Pie, Vegetables, including potatoes chipped, boiled, roasted, mashed, Sweets; cakes, pies, and various ice creams. Tea and bread, of course.

'I'll have 'Welsh Rabbit', please.'

She leaned forward to look at the BILL of FARE, and I pointed to the item.

'Oh,' she said. ''Welsh Rarebit'.'

I was puzzled by her pronunciation of 'rabbit', but I knew from my reading that restaurants used fancy titles for fairly common dinners.

'Will you have a pot of tea with your rarebit, sir? she asked.

'Yis, please. A pot of tea, thank you. And bread.'

She paused in her writing and looked up.

'Rarebit comes with bread, sir.'

'Oh, I said,' suddenly confused.

'Will that be all?' she asked.

'I'll have potatoes. And peas. Please.'

She frowned.

'We don't serve potatoes or vegetables with rarebit. Do you want soup and a sweet?'

She had dropped the 'sir', and spoke sharply. I squirmed; my ordering had taken an odd turn.

'No, no, just the rabbit and tea, thank you.'

She stared at me, then swung on her heel and left.

Relieved that she had gone, I turned to my neighbours. They had frozen, their knives and forks poised over their plates. At my glance they thawed, and I leaned back in my chair.

It had been ages since I had eaten rabbit. Herbie didn't like it; he once said a dead rabbit looked like a skinned cat, and ever since, when I passed skinned rabbits in a butcher's shop window, I would wonder. I was curious about 'Welsh' rabbit.

Must come with leeks, or a special gravy. Maybe 'rarebit' is Welsh for rabbit; after all, Welsh is a language with a strange pronunciation.

Despite the confusion with the waitress over ordering potatoes and bread, I felt pleased with my choice, with a price that suited me.

Leaves me with quite a few bob. I can afford a new book or a few second-hand ones at Hugh Greer's in Smithfield Market. Put the rest in my Post Office savings book. Too late to use any of it to buy better presents. I could have bought Mammy something more expensive than a brooch from Woolworth's. A scarf, perhaps.

The discouraging warning about the stinginess of the Directors proved to be true. By mid-afternoon, I had scaled down my expectations because three of them had left by lunchtime without so much as a 'Merry Christmas' to us. Only Mr Marshall, Financial Secretary of the Board, remained. So far, I had received two bob each from Andre and the clerks to whom I delivered memos and mail and with whom I sometimes chatted. All told, quite short of the small fortune of my day-dreams.

At about four o'clock, our office phone rang. I overhead the Hall Porter: 'Yes, Mr Marshall, right away, sir.' The Hall Porter turned to the bench where my mates and I sat. 'Mr Marshall wants to see one of you. Willie, come on, hop to it.'

I liked Mr Marshall, a courteous man, even towards message boys. He was not stout and short, like Sir Frederick, but of medium height and build, handsome, with silver hair, and tanned faced and hands, which made me think he must spend more time on the French Riviera than at the shipyard.

When I entered his office, he was standing behind his desk with an open gold cigarette case in his hand, and for a daft moment I thought he was going to offer me a cigarette. The white cuffs of his shirtsleeves protruded beyond the sleeves of his light grey suit; the fingers of his right hand were heavily stained by nicotine. He lit a cigarette. Smoke curled from his mouth and nose, wreathing his face like wisps of white hair.

'The Sergeant sent you?' he asked.

Everybody, except messenger boys, called the porter, 'The Sergeant'. An ex-serviceman, he wore three chevrons of the Corps of Commissionaires.

'Yes sir,' I replied.

'Your name is…'

'Morrison,' I supplied.

This was the first time in the seven months I had been running errands for him that he had asked me my name.

He came out from behind his desk, crossed the floor to a cabinet, and pulled out a bottom drawer. It brimmed with money in rows of neatly bundled new notes: ten shilling, pound, and fivers big enough to write a letter on. I stared, wide-eyed. *No shilling Christmas boxes here. It would be notes.* My earlier expectations revived. He bent down to the drawer.

'How many boys does the Sergeant have?' he asked, half turning towards me.

'Three, sir.'

He peeled a note off a bundle, gave it to me, and closed the drawer. It was a pound. Twenty shillings. *Three into twenty won't go*. But I said nothing.

'Merry Christmas, Mr Morrison.'

'Merry Christmas, sir.'

On my way back to the office, my mind buzzed with more than mental arithmetic. For a wild moment in front of that open drawer I had thought that Mr Marshall was going to peel three pound notes from a bundle. He could have tossed me a whole bundle, and it wouldn't have been missed. Still, a pound note was better than nothing.

The Sergeant solved the problem of division by changing the pound into shillings from a tin box in which he kept tips from visitors. He added a shilling to make the pound a guinea, so that we would be equally satisfied; seven bob apiece. Before we scattered for home, he gave each of us a half-crown.

My Christmas boxes fell short of the haul other office messengers claimed to have taken, which ranged from thirty bob to two or three quid, if they were to be believed. I may not have had enough for a decent game of pitch and toss, as one wag taunted, but I was satisfied. I had been within two paces of real wealth, and I would remember that sight long after they had forgotten how they had spent their thirty bobs and three pounds.

A waitress with a tray held aloft in one hand interrupted my reverie. She set a cup and saucer, a pot of tea, a small sugar bowl and small jug of milk at my right hand. I leaned away from her as she laid a plate between my knife and fork. On the plate an orange puddle flecked with black pustules was slowly congealing. I looked at it in dismay. Thin strands of steam rose from the plate and evaporated, and my appetite with them.

The waitress was about to turn away.

'Miss. Miss,' I said. 'I asked for rabbit.'

She looked at me, her face expressionless.

'That's rarebit,' she replied. 'That's what you asked for.'
Her voice was sharp again.

'But it's not rabbit,' I protested.

'It's RAREBIT, sir,' she said. 'Rarebit is cheese on toast. You ordered cheese on toast.'

I was about to protest that I didn't want cheese on toast because I hated cheese, but she had left me and was sashaying between the tables towards the kitchen. I studied the BILL of FARE closely. Sure enough, it said 'Rarebit'.

I looked down at the offensive excuse for a dinner now glued to my plate. I never ate cheese; I couldn't stand its smell of decay nor its sour taste. The couple beside me were quietly laughing. Suddenly, my annoyance at my mistake gave way to an awful sensation. My face burned as if I had held it close to red hot coals, and I began to sweat. I looked at the restaurant door, but didn't move.

Since I was paying for the rarebit, I ate it, bite by torturous bite, washing each disgusting morsel down my reluctant gullet with tea, which, at least, steadied my nerves and cooled my sudden feverishness. The restaurant had lost its festive air, and the chatter had become raucous.

When I had eaten, I signalled to the waitress.

'Could I have my bill, please?'

She pulled a small book and pencil from her apron pocket, jotted something, tore the page out, and placed it on the table. I picked it up. 'Welsh Rarebit', 'Pot of Tea', and opposite each, the cost.

'There's a mistake here, Miss. You've added in th' price of th' tea,' I said.

'The menu is 'A La Carte'. That means you pay for each item,' she replied.

I picked up the BILL of FARE. Like a gospel text printed boldly above the platform in a gospel hall, 'A La Carte' convicted me of further ignorance, and I felt my temperature rise again. I muttered:

'So I have t' pay for th' tea?'

She didn't answer.

I paid her, and when she left I shoved a sixpence beneath the plate which still bore traces of my humiliation. Without as much as a glance at my neighbours, I left the table, unhooked my still sodden overcoat, and fled the restaurant. The Albert Clock chimed the quarter hour. I glanced up. A quarter to seven.

If only I could roll yer flippin' hands back an hour an' begin again, I told myself. I turned to the restaurant where I had made a fool of myself. I vowed never to enter it again, and hastened to catch a tram for home.

On the tram's upper deck I took a seat a seat by a window and hunched into my damp overcoat like a chastened child smarting from a spanking. Condensation on the tram's windows hid the world moving by me. The fact that I had learned a thing or two in the restaurant, that I wouldn't make such a fool of myself again, did little to ease my bruised pride, but I had one small consolation; the restaurant did not have waiters like Andre.

An image of a drawer full of bundled notes intruded on my brooding, and my heaviness began to lighten a little.

Now, there's a story t'tell. Ye know, I could'av coshed Marshall there and then, but not too hard for he's a decent man, an' stuffed bundles of pounds into my pockets an' bundles of fivers inside my shirt.
I let my imagination rip:
I'd walk out of the Main Office, for I'd no longer need my flipping job, nor flippin' Christmas boxes from directors, an' take a boat to America, an' forget about flippin' Welsh rarebit an' bloody rabbits an' flippin' waitresses with cloth tiaras perched on their heads.

I pulled myself up straight in the seat, and with the sleeve of my coat cleared a hole in the condensation on the window and peered out.

The tram rattled and swayed its way up the Crumlin Road, veered on to the Oldpark, stopping often to pick up and drop passengers, most homeward bound, I fancied, some bearing gifts bought in the dying hours of this holy Eve. At Oldpark Avenue, a short distance from where I usually got off, the tram stopped again. At the corner of the avenue a broad shaft of familiar light fell across the footpath. On an impulse, I dashed down the stairs from the upper deck and leaped off the tram just as it had begun to move again. In three bounds I was at the fish and chip shop. Its door swung easily inwards.

With a warm parcel held under my arm I set off for home. After walking several yards I peeled the newspaper wrapping open to draw a chip from the greasy tangle underneath a piece of golden swaddled fish. An aroma of grease and vinegar arose in the night air. I breathed deeply, and picked up the pace of my stride. My humiliation in the restaurant still rankled, but my heart grew lighter with every steady footfall toward home, with every tinkle of silver against my thigh, with every prospect of the happy day ahead.

The drizzle that had persisted all day into the early evening had ceased, as if the sky had given up trying to rain. The mirk was thinning too, so that clusters of stars became visible in the deeps of the sable sky, some brighter than others.

Welsh rabbit indeed! Mammy will have a good laugh when I tell her about my ignorance. 'Flipsy flu,' she'll say, 'an' yous thinkin' you'll be getting a stew. Ye must be starvin'.' I'll laugh too, and say I'm not. And over a glass of ginger wine she will have made for this holy night, I'll tell her about the drawer full of money, and as usual, hand her an unopened pay packet. And I'll tell her 'Keep it all, Mammy, for this time I have my Christmas boxes.'

Chapter 18

AN ISLANDMAN

I

The early winter morning was bleak and dismal. I could have taken a tram from downtown's Castle Junction to the 'Yard, and for a while longer have been dozy and snug, but like my father, I was in the habit of walking this stretch of the road to the Island.

We didn't always walk to work together. Usually, he left the house while I was dithering about the kitchen to delay my exit into the cold, but on that morning we caught the downtown tram together, and hoofed the mile or so from the city's centre to the shipyard.

Except for the hours spent under the same roof at home, he and I inhabited different worlds. I was deeply religious, and had pulled away from his more worldly existence, having no more interest in the horse racing at Aintree than he had in the prayer meeting I had attended the previous night. Yet, though we talked little as we walked, I was comfortable keeping pace with him, and he gave me no reason to think that it was otherwise with him.

At the gate to the Engine Works, he swung away from me. 'Be careful,' he said, and disappeared through the gate, while I carried on toward the Musgrave Channel, where the *Juan Peron* was moored.

In the cold half-light, the boat's black hull towered like the granite wall of a canyon above the men gathering on the wharf. Elsewhere, the grey of breaking day had begun to thin the darkness, but here gloom lingered, draped like a veil over time-huts, wooden crates, mounds of rubbish, a litter of pipes, paint and oil drums, and over the figures that moved among them. An arc lamp on the boat's main deck sprayed light towards the wharf, the effect exaggerating rather than alleviating the melancholy aspect of the place, so that, as I joined a line of men shunting past the lighted window of a hut, I shuddered, as if to shake off the gloom, as I would shake rain of my coat, and turned my coat collar up about my neck, although I wasn't cold.

We always walked briskly, my father and I. And said little. It had been like that since our first walk together to the shipyard on the morning I began to serve my time.

He had insisted, in the mild manner he had of getting his way, that my brother and I 'serve our time'. He didn't have a trade. Not having any other ambition when I left school, I fell in with his wish. Poring over the list on Harland and Wolff's application form one late spring evening after dinner, we quickly passed over Blacksmith, Driller, Plater, Riveter, Welder, Sheet metal Worker. ('Heavy trades, son. Dirty work,' he said.) At seven stone, fully clothed, boots on, I would be lifted off my feet swinging a sledgehammer. I hovered over Electrician, Pattern-maker, Shipwright. He muttered objections. Near the bottom of the list appeared Woodworker, and he said: 'Yer uncle Joe's a joiner. Clean trade. Wud suit ye.' How? I wondered. Did he mean my build or temperament? I was small, slight, and occasionally bothered by the combination. Temperament, I decided.

When I received a letter telling me to report to the Foreman's Office at the Joiners' Shop for an interview, he advised me: 'Polish yer shoes before ye go, don't put yer hands in yer pockets nor lean against th' wall while yer waitin' for th' foreman. Ye don't want Mr McGrath, the head foreman, thinkin' yur a corner boy.' The advice gave me the jitters about the interview, and, I thought later, unnecessarily so, for judging by the appearances of some of the other boys also being interviewed on the same morning, and who, like me, were admitted to the apprenticeship, I doubted whether my deportment had any effect on Mr McGrath.

I bound myself for five years to Harland and Wolff's Limited. The Indenture read like a page out of the Book of Leviticus. I covenanted that I would 'diligently and faithfully... serve the Employers, keep their secrets, willingly and diligently obey their lawful commands... not absent (myself) without permission from the Employers' service; but shall in all things behave as a faithful Apprentice ought to do...' Should I 'be guilty of disobedience, misconduct, or disrespect towards the Employers, their manager, or any foreman, or of vicious or immoral conduct…' I may be sacked or suspended, and would forfeit my bond-money of five pounds sterling.

The bond was a princely sum to me – in fact, anything above five shillings was a fortune – because there wasn't that much money in my mother's purse, nor in my father's pocket, nor in my Post Office Savings Account. An uncle, my mother's brother, paid it. When he handed me the large white note he said, 'Pay me back when ye come out of yer time.' For an instant, I thought of eternity.

On the first morning of my 'time' I marched alongside my father in my unblemished navy dungarees, whose bib buttons gleamed like new farthings. He walked quickly, his shoulders slightly swaying as if he was swimming against the air. My stiff dungarees slapped against my shins like cardboard and the heels of my boots clacked bold trochees against the concrete footpath. I carried a large shining tea can, which declared, as clearly as a placard, that I was not a seasoned Islandman.

When we reached the gates of the Engine Works, my father spoke:

'Ye'll be awright, nigh, son?'

His question, an assertion in disguise, reassured me – as it was meant to.

'Yis, Daddy.'

'When ye git yur board, keep it in th' tap pocket of yur coat where it'll nat git lost. Take care o'yerself, nigh.'

Whatever he felt, I didn't know, but I think he was pleased.

'Yis,' I answered, and picked up the pace again toward my destiny.

The year rolled along, slowly, like a cart of pig-iron hauled by a Clydesdale. I learned the rudiments of my trade, how to use the tools. I sand papered miles of cabin moulding, and kept the squad's glue pot hot, and ran fool's errands for smirking journeymen.

It was customary for apprentices to spend their second year on the boats. Most joiners in the Shop hated them. Dirty and dangerous, they said. But by the end of my green year, I was ready for any boat, dirt and danger be damned, and I waited expectantly for the call. When Moffatt, my gaffer, on one of his hawk-eyed patrols stopped at my bench, leaned toward me and said, 'Willie, yer fer th' boats,' I grinned as if he had given me a week's holiday. He paused to make sure I had heard him rightly before he added the name of a boat:

'*Juan Peron*. Number Two Quay on Musgrave Channel.' I held the grin, but my pleasure dipped a few degrees in temperature, then steadied.

At dinner I told my father:

'I'm fer the *Juan Peron* on Monday.'

'What sort a work are ye goan be doin'?'

'Buildin' th' crew's cabins. Nat much fine joinery in her.' I didn't tell him that joiners scorned whale-factory ships, because their crew's quarters were furnished with wardrobes, bunks, and dressers made by tinsmiths; it might disappoint him, as I was disappointed, that I was being sent to a whaling boat rather than a fancy passenger liner like the *Rhodesia Castle*.

'She's the biggest whale-factory ship in th' world,' I said, as if in compensation for the loss of the *Rhodesia Castle*.

He nodded, his eyes twinkled with amusement. He became serious.

'Watch out fer holes in decks, ye don't fall down thim. An' keep an eye on what's above ye when yer climbin' them lahers, son.' His lazy Ligoniel pronunciation of 'ladders' grated on me. I didn't admit to him that the prospect of having to climb ladders every day scared and yet titillated me, like a dare a boy accepts to climb a dangerous tree because he knows the deed will bolster his self-esteem, especially if he is small and slight. My father knew of the hazards of working on boats only by report, and I felt that in my prospect of having to face them every day I had surpassed him in some way.

If his remark about the dangers of working on the boats made my mother anxious for my safety, she concealed it.

'Ye'll be needin' yer dungaroos again, I suppose,' she said to me.

For the past months, I had worn a shop joiner's apron.

'Yis.'

'Well, th're still hingin' in th' hall, an' should still fit ye,' she said. Whatever my pretensions, she had the measure of them; I was still a wee lad.

At the *Juan Peron*, on the first morning of my first year on the boats, I was awestruck by its height above the wharf. The boat's boarding deck was reached by two gangways. One spanned the wharf and a platform rigged at right angles to the ship's hull about twenty feet above the wharf; the other, wide as a staircase, arose alongside the hull from the lower platform to meet another extending from the main deck. Its height, at high tide, must have been at least fifty feet above the wharf.

I hoisted my heavy toolbox on to my right shoulder, steadied it against the side of my head, and heart thumping, gripped a handrail with my free hand to begin my ascent of the gangways. At each step, my legs shimmied like a greyhound's flanks. As I climbed, I could see the fender and the tract of oily sea water between the wharf and the boat's hull fall further away below me. My shoulder ached, but I dared not slacken my grip of the handrail, so that I might swing the box on to my other shoulder. Nor did I pause, for at the slightest hesitation in my climb my legs trembled. At the top of the gangway, I swung the toolbox on to the deck.

Breathless and pleased with myself, my kneecaps executing a jig, I leaned over the bulwark. Far below, in the water between the boat and the wharf, a long gridlock fender of large squared timbers gently bobbed in the slight swell of the Channel, nudging the ship's hull and the wharf's pilings.

There came mornings when I wished I had elsewhere to go than to the *Juan Peron*, and evenings when I was eager to leave the boat, but on most days I thrived on board, borne along not only by the skills I was acquiring but also by a pride in my trade. I had no regrets about my father's gentle persuasion.

And, no blot had stained my indenture nor jeopardised my bond, and no seagull soiled my duncher.

The shuffle of the line ahead brought me to the time-hut window. I called out my number through the rat-hole, and a timekeeper drew from the tray in front of him my board, a small thin block of wood, and slapped it down on the narrow window ledge. The board was old, worn and stained, and I wondered sometimes, if it had belonged to an Islandman now dead. I checked the five digits stamped on its end wood, shoved it into the bib pocket of my dungarees, and sauntered towards the gangway.

Men loitered, or sat wherever they could find a low crate, or a plank thrown across empty paint drums, or on the bollards at the wharf's edge. Cigarettes alternately glowed brightly and faded, like tiny red lamps transmitting a code through the gloom. I had no pocket watch to measure the minutes of grace before sirens whined and hooters blared all over the 'Yard's vast expanse, after which the timekeepers would shut the rat holes in the windows, often without clemency, shutting out latecomers from a day's pay. Rather than linger on the wharf, I followed a straggle of men boarding the boat. Underfoot, the gangway vibrated, gently, discordantly. On the boat an odour of oil, sea water, and stale welding fumes hung in the air.

I made my way along the main deck to the forward hold, stepping carefully across a serpentine network of black welders' cables and drillers' hoses, like a child avoiding the devil's cracks in a footpath. At the forward hold, I swung my legs over the hatch combing on to a forty-foot ladder, and descended into the dim belly of the ship. I no longer feared long ladders, though a ladder's shimmy under my weight always sent a flutter of anxiety through me.

On the refrigeration deck in the hold, my work mates sat about on tool boxes and low stools knocked together from plywood. Their greetings were low, terse, some just a nod. I replied in kind, and sat on my toolbox, content not to have to talk.

The hold felt like a dank cold crypt. Heat from the low watt temporary lights strung across the deck head had little effect on the chilly air. Everything one touched was ice cold: the steel deck overhead and underfoot, the hull. The steel breathed icily on one's face and hands, and seeped through the soles of boots. Even the asbestos sheets, nailed to studs bolted to the boat's ribs, had the smooth coldness of an effigy on a tomb.

Fifteen minutes or so after I sat down, a riveter's hammer rattled somewhere on the boat, like a heavy machine-gun opening a battle, and in the hold a welder and burner followed his lead, for within seconds the white flash of a welding rod splintered the grey light into blue-white triangles and rhomboids, and an acetylene torch sent a shower of red and gold sparks into the maw of the hold, some striking and dying on the planks by which we reached the ladder. My mates rose to their feet, opened their toolboxes, and soon hand saws rasped against bone hard asbestos sheets, and hammers rang tunelessly on nails. Two masked insulators, in boiler suits smeared with white chalk, bobbed among the overhead pipes. Flakes of insulation like fake snow fell to the deck. The hold began to reek of asbestos. Minute by minute, the morning worked its way toward noon, toward the stillness of lunch hour.

On the wharf below, steam rose from boilers which contained hot water for tea. I was the squad's tea-boy, and with two fistfuls of tea cans, I weaved my way down the crowded upper gangway, until I reached its midsection, at about the thirteenth or fourteenth step. Chat and banter rippled among us while we waited for the lunchtime hooter to blow. The gangway creaked loudly, and an unctuous voice intoned:

'From the dangers of this day, O Lord God, preserve us.'

There was a burst of laughter. Some men swore. A fellow at my elbow opined:

'Wudn't take much fer't t' go, it's so aul. Musta bin aroun' when they built th' *Titanic*. Juss a fuggan' hair crack in a stringer, that's all's boys, an' down we go, like spuds from the arse of a burst beg.'

More laughter. A hooter blared, and the gangway shuddered with our clattering.

Darkness had fallen when, in the late afternoon close to quitting time, I clambered off the ladder and over the hatch combing. Arc-lamps threw a strong light across the main deck and down the upper gangway. The boat was still, and only the coughs of men loitering in the shadows of the mid ship passageways disturbed the quiet.

A few painters, recognisable from their paint-stained overalls, stood near the gangway. I expected to see the 'hard hat', the boat's manager, behind them, for he usually stood at the head of the gangway to discourage men from leaving the boat too soon. Anyone attempting to slip by him risked the sack. He wore a bowler hat, as did all managers and shop foremen. It was believed that the crowns of these hats were reinforced with steel, because, it was rumoured, a worker might drop 'accidentally' a heavy tool, or rivets, or a large bolt, on a manager's head. But he was nowhere in sight.

His absence was a matter of indifference to me, because I had a pass from my gaffer, which allowed me to leave the boat early. I skipped down the empty gangway, slid my board and pass through a time-hut window to a clerk, and raced toward Queen's Road for the nearest tram going my way home. On the tram, I hunched into a doze, my head cradled in my duncher against the tram's window, which, from the dampness of the evening, glistened with condensation.

I was relieved to get off the boat fifteen minutes ahead of the crowd that usually filled the upper gangway ten minutes before the hooter blared. Earlier in the day, I had thought that I would join them, and as at lunchtime, worm my way close to its bottom step, so that at the first blast of the hooter, I might bolt for the waiting trams. But I had changed my mind.

If my elocution class had not been switched from Saturday to the Wednesday by the tutor 'for one session only' I would not have been in the dilemma that had bothered me on boarding the boat that morning: whether to slip off among the painters or to ask Norm, the gaffer, for a pass, even though that would mean revealing a secret I had kept from my mates.

For three weeks now, I had been stretching my mouth wide in all directions, ejaculating vowels until my jaw ached, and picking pecks of pickled peppers with Peter Piper to feed soldiers waiting for sister Susie to sew their shirts. My mates knew nothing of my pursuit of perfect diction; I was not eager to acquire a nickname, like 'La-di-da', which would spread throughout the boat at the rate of a highly contagious infection, and pass into shipyard lore. Everyone, including those who never met him, knew Shout, a wee man who always whispered in your ear, Low Watt, a dim fellow, Nosey, who had a grotesque growth on his nose, and, indeed, La-di-da, a joiner in the Shop whose first name was Lennie.

'Ye mean yer learning t'talk fancy, Willie? Hoity-toity like? Like them fuggan hard hats? Gitin' airs about yourself, Willie?'

I had no reason for taking elocution, no ambitions to be an orator or actor. Two friends, one of whom aspired to the Presbyterian ministry, had arranged to meet weekly with a teacher who, for a small fee, offered to teach them elocution and English composition, and I tagged along, believing that any improvement in my speech and writing would do me no harm.

The rocking motion of the tram drew me easily into sleep, and I dozed until the furious clanging of a bell pulled me out of it. I rubbed a clearing in the condensation, and saw an ambulance race by. Murmurs purled among the passengers. I settled back to sleep, unaware that my solution to my dilemma may have saved my life, and unaware too, that on the wharf alongside the *Juan Peron,* my father was frantically searching among the faces of the dead and the living for the familar face of his son.

Chapter 19

THE BOND

MY FATHER rarely spoke about that dreadful night and I cannot tell my story without telling his.

With the flow of the tide on the last night of January, 1951, the giant *Juan Peron* rode high above the wharf of Number Two Quay, higher than any other vessel in the Musgrave Channel at the Belfast shipyard. Beneath its upper gangway, for it took two gangways to board the ship's main deck, a fender – a honeycombed raft of large square timbers set into cross beams – gently rubbed, now against the ship's hull, now against the wharf's piles, in the Channel's slight swell. Night had fallen, and the winter air – it was the last day of January – was noticeably colder.

Workers waiting for the blast of the hooter to send them homeward had wedged themselves solid on the upper gangway. It complained sharply, and men laughed as if they expected it to groan, for it always groaned under their weight, and yet expected nothing from it. The laughter lingered like a chord extended on a piano, and the men – among them at least two youths, hardly older than boys – hunched against the cold damp. Anyway, if you heard a warning in the groan, you were powerless to heed it; in the crush of a hundred or so bodies only those on the bottom step could move to safety.

Another creak, louder this time, snapped against the night. A few nervous curses rippled down the gangway, and faded into a hush, an expectant hush, as if the men were on a terrace in a football ground watching a player step forward to take a decisive penalty shot.

The gangway shuddered, and now the men sensed danger. 'She's givin'! She's givin'!' someone shouted. There was no panic, for there was no time to panic; the gangway, with a 'Bang' like the crack of an artillery cannon, snapped in two.

Surprised by the terror of the steps under them falling away, as if a trapdoor had been sprung beneath them, men grabbed for ropes in the air. Finding none, they clutched each other and plunged together toward the wharf and water and fender below, all but one spilling like mannequins from a burst sack. Their screams of protest were swallowed by the crash of the lower section of the gangway hitting the fender. A black air-hose, severed by the falling debris, roared with an infernal hiss.

As though at an abrupt wave of an unseen hand, the crashing and screaming ceased. The top half of the broken gangway, still hinged to its steel platform, its stringers and handrail splintered, swung slightly, creaked, and came to rest. For a moment only the monstrous hiss of the air-hose could be heard, then slowly, like an undertone in a dirge sung off-stage, moans and whimpers and cries of injured and dying men arose from below the edge of the wharf.

On the far side of the road opposite the quay, workers bound homeward from other ships and shops tramped by, noting only, at the edge of their consciousness, the familiar hissing of a fractured air-hose.

Against their flow a man in his early forties ran erratically, dodging instinctively the dark forms trudging toward him, until he reached Number Two Quay.

His heart hammered from his exertion. And from fear.

His son, a young lad, worked on the *Juan Peron*.

At the Engine Works, minutes earlier, at 5.31pm, to be precise, my father Billy Morrison, had reached the time-office, when he heard his foreman shout. He tossed his board through the rat-hole in the window, and turned back into the warehouse, irritated.

'What's he want nigh? Th' bloody hooter went a minute ago.'

'Bin a bad accident at th' Musgrave Channel, Billy,' his foreman said.

'Where? What boat?'

'Number Two quay. The *Juan Peron*. Yer lad's on it, int he?'

Billy nicked the cigarette he had lit on leaving the warehouse, and at a half run, made for the east gate of the Engine Works. Fitters, machinists, pattern makers, foundry men and labourers were streaming out of the machine shops and foundries into the alleys between the buildings. As if in pursuit of a pickpocket, he dodged, sidestepped, nudged aside the bodies that slowed down his progress toward the gate. Once through, moving now against the flow of men tramping home along the Channel road, he broke into a trot. Down the road the black bluff of the *Juan Peron*'s bow rose above the quay into the night, and he lengthened his stride.

The quay was half-lit, like a set for a melodrama. Shafts of light from the open doors of time-huts and from the headlights of ambulances pushed yellow corridors through the darkness. Nearby, a ruptured air hose hissed like an infernal monster disturbed in its den. An arc-lamp, hanging halfway down the ship's side, splayed an inverted funnel of light down the hull toward the water below. Men crouched at the wharf's edge, and now and again straightened up, in their grasp a limp form which they carried to a nearby stretcher. Shouts echoed the same refrain: 'Hing on me bye, we'll git ye out!' Billy could hear, like the undertone of a dirge off-stage, moans, whimpers, calls for help rising from the water between the boat and the wharf.

'In God's name what's happened?' he called out to no-one in particular.

'Up thonder,' a voice answered, and the speaker's arm swung toward the platform on the main deck of the ship.

'Bloody gangway broke. Snapped in two. Men came down wi' it, spillin' like rivets out a burst beg. Most piled on th' fender, so them as fell first had no chance, th' weight shoved th' fender deep in th' water. Some fellas wis catapulted by th' gangway swingin' an' missed th' fender an' went in th' wather, an' some hit th' wharf's edge, like one fella who landed on them bollards. He lay there like a broke doll.'

Billy glanced at the twin bollards a few yards to the left of him, and then looked up at the gangway. Its top half dangled from the platform, the jagged splinters of its broken stringers pointing toward the water below. The handrails were split like kindlin' under a hatchet.

'God almighty!' he whispered.

Taking his cue from the mild oath, his companion pointed again to the gangway:

'An at th' thirteenth step too, ye wudn't believe it.' Billy didn't check the observation – which, indeed, was true – for he was seized by a dread that had nothing to do with superstition. He peered again toward the boat's main deck. A row of pale faces lined its bulwark, each inscrutable against the darkness. He tried to discern his son's among them, but could not.

He turned his attention to the activity on the wharf. By the light of the arc-lamp rescuers lifted moaning and limp bodies up toward hands reaching down for them from the wharf's lip. An experienced St John Ambulance man, he began to assist the rescuers.

His preoccupation with the injured eased the clamp around his chest. The dead were laid at random in the shadows of the time-huts, and he felt a momentary, though guilty, relief when he failed to recognise a familiar face. Finding a fellow propped up against the wall of a time-hut, duncher slightly askew on his head, Billy lit a cigarette, took a draw, and put it in the fellow's mouth. The cigarette dangled from the still lips, a thin trail of smoke curling about the half-open eyes, and Billy removed the feg, stubbed it, and gently closed the fellow's eyes. 'Not a mark on him.' he marvelled to himself. 'Smothered.'

So far, he had not seen his son, nor any sign of him. His anxiety abated a little, for, he told himself, this absence increases the odds that the lad is still on the ship. When the last of the injured had been taken off in an ambulance, he joined a few men at the wharf's edge. Below them the fender, relieved of its unexpected burden, rocked easily again on the tide; films of sea water seeped over it, washing away traces of blood. Debris from the lower part of the gangway floated nearby. The water gleamed like polished ebony, implacable, except for the reflection of the arc-lamp, a yellow disc, like a sun floating unaccountably on the heave of night.

The men beside him spoke in subdued tones:

'Did they git iverybody?'

'God knows how many went in th' water, maybe goin' under the wharf.'

'Divers nat goin' down 'til th'morn, so they say.'

The conversation brought back the intensity of his fear, and like a gambler listening to a horse race where he has staked his wages, he could feel impending loss. At the wharf's edge, he scanned the alley of water between the ship and the wharf, and out where it broadened into the darkness. He looked up again at the pale faces bent over the ship's side, hoping that one of them might recognise him in the yellow light, and shout. He would recognize easily the high pitch, not yet a man's. But the faces were silent. An astonishing story by one of his companions distracted him for a moment.

It appeared that a fellow, standing at the inside handrail when the gangway broke, instinctively had grabbed hold of a thick steel plate welded to the ship's side, and had held on as the gangway swung away beneath his feet.

'He wis hingin' just a few feet below the top of the ship's side, by his figgers!' the informant exclaimed. 'Ye cud hear th' fellas on the deck shoutin' at him 'Hing on, hing on nigh, we'll git ye up'. Then somedee on th' main deck wis lower'd upside down o'er th' side 'til he reached 'im an' was able t' grab 'is wrists, an' then the both wis pulled up on t' th' deck. God knows wha' went on in th' poor bugger's head, hingin' there by his figgers, tiring by th' second.'

'Jesus. Brave man, him who went over the side to git 'im,' one of the listeners interjected.

'Ay, an' held by his feet, so he was, by his mates,' another added. At this, a whispering of blasphemies, like quiet prayers, passed among them.

There was nothing more Billy could do but wait until another gangway replaced the broken one, and the rest of the workers disembarked. He paced up and down the wharf to ease the tension tightening his body. His mind leapt from possibility to possibility. If the lad doesn't come down the gangway, he thought, then he's probably in one of the hospitals. He hadn't been able to keep track of the injured. 'Sixty or so hurted,' somebody had said. 'Eighty,' said another. He had asked ambulance crews if they had picked up any young lads, and someone had mentioned two, but the descriptions didn't fit his son.

When the new gangway arrived and was set in place, Billy stood close to it while the workmen filed down. Now and again he thought he had seen his son stepping on to it, but was mistaken. The flow thinned to a trickle, and finally a manager, who had boarded the boat just as the gangway had been placed, appeared. When he reached the wharf, Billy stepped towards him.

'Is nobody else up there, sir?' he asked, nodding to the boat.

'Are you looking for someone?' the manager replied.

'Young lad. Me son.'

'Everybody's off. Are you sure he was on the ship?'

'Yis. He worked on't. Him an' me left th' house toge'er this morn.'

Company officials, newspaper men, workers, were gathering around the manager, and Billy moved away. He could feel a panic rising within himself. Maybe the lad had taken ill, left the boat early. But he had been fine this morning, he told himself. If the lad's not in a hospital, there's only one place left. The water, maybe floating under the wharf. His worst thought, but he steadied himself. Better get home, he muttered to himself, then do the rounds of hospitals. Mabel will be up the walls, wondering what's keeping the lad and me. He cursed the fact that they had no telephone, nor did anybody on the street, as far as he knew. Even so, the 'phone wouldn't make any easier the task he really dreaded.

Only an infrequent tram ran along Queen's Road, and rather than wait for one, he decided to walk back into the city centre. He lit another cigarette.

He walked with quick short steps, his usual stride, his shoulders rolling in rhythm with each step. He was used to walking fast in his job as runner between the Engine Works and the Lagan Docks, but his thighs and calves now ached. Beyond the Engine Works the road was poorly lit. Lamp posts, spaced like sentinels down the middle of the road, cast light on the twin sets of tram lines, but threw the footpaths on either side into shadow.

The darkness thickened where he cut by the loading bays for Kelly's coal boats at the Abercorn Basin. Black pyramids of coal, like a low range of hills, lined the quayside, their silhouettes barely distinguishable from the night sky above them. Though dampness had kept dust from rising about his feet as he walked, he could taste bitter carbon on his lips. The air smelled as though sieved through a screen of soot.

His mind churned the images of what he had seen in the last three hours, and images of his son, of his wife and his other children, all recurring as in a dream, connecting and disconnecting. He shook his head, held his tears from spilling. That it should come to this. Should have kept the lad out of the 'Yard. Out of harm's way. Mabel didn't want him working there in the first place.

It didn't seem so long ago – five years now – that he thought he had lost his other son, Norman. Wee lad of eleven. Ruptured appendix. It was touch and go, the poison spreading through his body, and the doctors' hoping for the new wonder drug, penicillin, to stop the creep of death. It did, thank God. But the agony of waiting was almost unendurable. Hit Mabel hard, it did. But this is going to be worse. 'Missing, presumed…' Isn't that how it's put?

Across the river, the Albert Clock chimed.

Within minutes he reached the Queen's Bridge. Lamp posts simpered on the bridge's low walls, their fading haloes shimmering on wet footpaths and scattering into glistening atoms on the black water of the River Lagan below as it crawled towards its end in the deeps of the Lough. He glanced towards the Queen's Quay. The Heysham and Liverpool boats dozed alongside the deserted docks before their plod across the Irish Sea. At bridge end he entered Ann Street, walking through whiffs of stale stout draughting from the doorways of half-lit public houses, passing bookie shops now shut up like bank vaults. He turned right into Victoria Street.

At the corner he looked up at the Albert. Past nine o'clock. He could hear the exasperation as well as anger in her voice. She'd put his lateness down to his thoughtlessness: 'goin' to that flippin' St John Ambulance without tellin' me before ye left this morning.' But this time her son is late too.

A trio of trams clustered around Castle Junction. He spotted one bound for the Oldpark Road, and changed his stride to a trot. On the tram, he was glad of the chance to sit after the walk, to rest himself, to collect his wits which, while he had walked, had flitted about his brain like sparrows trapped under a roof. He lit another cigarette, noted his packet low.

It was a ten-minute walk from where he got off the tram to the street where he lived. Now that he was close to home, he could feel panic swamping his body. 'What am I t'tell Mabel? Must find the right words,' he muttered to himself, 'find the right words.' His racing brain propelled him forward, but at times the full burden of his predicament almost pressed him physically to his knees. Sentences forming in his head fell into incoherent jumbles, like letters spilled from a child's alphabet box. He flung away the butt of his cigarette. By the time he reached the street where he lived, he could barely contain himself, his inarticulate anguish pressing sorely on his heart, so that he could scarcely breathe.

At the front door he tried to compose himself while he drew the house key on its string out through the letterbox, and opened the door. Without hanging his coat in the hallway, he went into the kitchen.

Mabel was waiting for him, her worry, at the sound of the key in the lock, converted to anger and her tongue ready to lash out at him. When she saw his white face, his stricken eyes, his unsteadiness, she knew right away that a St John Ambulance meeting had not kept him late, nor drink, though he was not a drinking man.

'In God's name, what's wrong wi' ye? Ye should see yerself.'
He looked at the clock, not into the mirror over the mantelpiece. It was almost ten, three and a half hours after he and his son usually got home from the shipyard. She hadn't mentioned her son.

'Is Will home yit?' he asked in a low voice, trying to sound casual. Surprised by the question, she pointed to the hallway:

'Did ye nat see his dungaroos?' she said, her voice sharp with scorn. He looked into the hallway, and then sat heavily on the sofa. The agony about to convulse him poured out in a long sigh, and he began to tell her of his night.

II

The hour was late when I arrived home from the elocution class, and I was surprised that my parents had not gone to bed. I hung my overcoat beside my dungarees in the hallway, and went into the kitchen. The fire in the grate was low, a dull red.

'It's a flippin' miracle yer here,' my mother said.

I thought she was being sarcastic about my coming home late, but her quiet tone puzzled me. Then my father spoke:

'Sit down, son. I've something t'tell ye.'

When he finished his brief account of the accident, I asked if he heard the names of the dead and injured. He shook his head. 'Mostly 'red-leaders',' he said, the painters who slap red paint on every exposed inch of steel on the boat, and, it seems, on every exposed inch of skin on their hands, arms and faces, and who are, accordingly, allowed to leave the boat early. He nodded towards the wireless in the kitchen nook:

'It's bin on th' wireless. Seventeen dead, as far as they know, 'bout eighty hurted. Don't know how many's missing, until youse all go in tamarra an' draw yer boords. So, you've t'go t'work as usual in th' morn.'

For a while we talked of the accident, of stricken families and their sudden unbearable grief. I told about the gangway, about it creaking at lunch time, and we speculated angrily on where blame should fall, because none of these men died through their own negligence, not from a fatal step off a staging nor a slip on a ladder nor a careless manoeuvre on a machine. As we talked, I was aware how much the bond between Islandmen was forged from the ever-present danger of our daily working lives.

Midnight passed. The fire in the grate was now dead, and the kitchen cold. My mother went to bed, leaving me with a gentle reminder to put out the kitchen light. After she had gone, my father, nodding toward the stairs, said in a low voice:

'I didn't know how I was goin t'tell yur mother I culdn't find ye. That wis the wurst. I cudn't find the words.'

I shifted my gaze from the hearth to his face. His eyes were wet. A sentiment took hold of me, which I did not articulate, nor even express in a gesture. Embarrassed, I told him about the dilemma I had been in, and how I had decided finally to get a pass from my gaffer.

'That wis right, son, what ye did,' he said.

Later, I lay in the darkness among the imagined sounds of a collapsing gangway and screams of falling men. I thought of my mates, and of my own escape, and my father's anxious search for me. And staring into darkness, I quietly wept.

The jagged sections of the gangway were still hanging from the platform, when I picked up my board on the morning after the disaster. An eerie stillness had settled on the boat, men moved silently and cautiously along the deck, as if afraid to disturb the stillness with their footfalls.

'Ye were lucky last night, Willie,' one of my mates said. Luck. Providence. I merely nodded, but my certainties had been shaken.

I learned that one of the insulation workers was killed, his mate badly injured, as was an apprentice joiner from another squad, who had tried to slip off the ship early among the painters.

Now and again the ladder into the hold creaked, like an old staircase in a house of mourning.

By midday, everyone was accounted for, including a missing red leader, who was found in the water. The evening newspaper *Belfast Telegraph* published the list of the dead, eighteen in all, some of them were men with young families, one fellow would have been married at Easter, another had been badly wounded twenty-five years earlier at the Battle of the Somme in the Great War, and yet another was a painter who lived on our street. I read the list aloud to my parents, naming names that were mostly unfamiliar to me, yet remembering what each name meant:

'J. Brackenridge, Edward Cullen, Russell Hamilton,
Walter Hurst, George Hynds, Robert James,
Fred Kernoghan, Robert McBride, Joseph McConnell,
Alan McCormick, Frank McMullen, W. J. Paterson,
John Patton, William Reid, John Shannon,
Robert Weatherall, David Weir and Archibald White.'

My elocution lessons came to an abrupt end, for a reason not related to these events. Throughout the remaining years of my apprenticeship I worked on other boats, doing rough and fine joinery, but I always felt relieved to be summoned back to a bench in the Joiners' Shop. Three and a half years later, I was summoned to the Head Foreman's office where I was handed my indenture. On it was written 'Apprenticeship Completed, 7/6/54', and with it my bond, a crisp white five pound note. Mr McGrath shook my hand. I had come 'out of my time'. At my uncle's request, my father bought me a watch with the bond money.

III

He and I never again talked about the accident. Our worlds, like our ways, parted several years later. I had decided to emigrate to Canada with my wife, Margaret, and our two young children. On the night of my departure – for I left in advance of them – my father came to see me off on the Liverpool steamer. He arrived late, just a few minutes before the steamer's doleful whistle warned visitors to leave the vessel. I had been searching for his face among the crowd on the quayside. As I pressed my way through the bodies thronging the narrow deck, I watched him make his way up the gangway. We met at its head. We had to shout to be heard above the din of voices. He asked me if my passport and wallet were secure in my inside pocket, and whether my travelling trunk was safely on board. Then he said:

'Must ye go? Cud ye nat stay here? Is there nat something for ye here?'

The questions had irritated me.

'It's better so, Daddy, a different life,' I answered.

I felt that I was deserting him. I was now a Presbyterian minister, and he was as proud of that as he was of his son, the joiner, always as proud of the one as of the other. That was the unspoken bond between us, I believed, and it occurred to me that by leaving for a new life in another country, I was, in a sense, betraying it.

The steamer's final impatient warning broke into the silence between us, as if in reproach for our dallying. We embraced, without awkwardness, and as he backed down towards the gangway, I was startled to see that he was weeping. At once, I saw that I had failed to grasp the true bond between us.

All my life I had known the strength of my mother's love for all her children; I had seen it in her tears, her anxiety in our illnesses, and felt it in the comfort of her embraces in our hurts. I knew too, that our father, he who mended our shoes, bandaged our wounds, advised us for our own good, cared for us. And I realised that the bond between my father and me had nothing to do with my accomplishments. It was there, as we children grew up, in the gestures of his blue eyes and shy smile, in the regularity

213

of his going to and coming home from work, in his worry when we were sick. It was like the simple furnishings of their kitchen house, which I knew would be still there when I came home from school or work, ever-present, and never given a second thought. It was there even in the care he took in choosing a watch for me.

And now, at the head of this gangway, which in a moment would be lifted, leaving him and me eventually on different shores, I had seen the strength of that bond. And a sadness beyond the sadness of parting, weighed upon me. I glanced at my watch, but couldn't clearly see the time.

'Take care o'yerself, nigh, son,' he shouted, swinging himself around at the top of the gangway to face me.

'I will, Dad. I'll be all right,' I shouted back.

I watched him go down the gangway in his rolling gait, feint his way through the crowd on the quay, and pass into the gloom of the loading shed. The steamer edged out into the middle of the River Lagan, and slipped past the shipyards into Belfast Lough. I stood a long time at the stern of the boat as the city between the mountains and the gantries slowly receded from me. At the moment they disappeared into the dusk, I turned to the open sea.

'Th' wurst for me,' he had said to me on that January night so long ago, 'wis on th' way home, I cudn't find th'words t'tell yer mother what might have happened to ye. Th' words just wuldn't come t'me.' The bond between us had been paid by him with an anguish which had left him inarticulate.

And now, with words, it might be redeemed.

ACKNOWLEDGEMENTS

I would like to express my thanks to all who made this book a labour of love:

To Francis Mansbridge, of Vancouver, British Columbia, former colleague, long-time friend and author, for his helpful comments on the stories when they were works in progress, and for encouraging me to seek their publication;

To Appletree Press and its editorial staff, Jean Brown, for her gracious editing, and Jim Black for his diligent copy-editing and Stuart Wilkinson for his design;

To my brother Norman, and sisters, Mavis and Elsie, all of Northern Ireland, who checked facts for me, corrected my recollection when it erred, offered tid-bits of their memories which often sparked my own, and, not least, welcomed the stories;

To my daughters, Grace, Clare, and Sarah, who heard fragments of the stories down the years at the dinner table and on vacations, and wanted me to continue the telling for their children;

And to my wife Margaret, for her love, patience, and countless cups of tea.

W.M.